H.I.T. or Miss

Lessons Learned from Health Information Technology Implementations

Editor: Jonathan Leviss, MD

Associate Editors:
Brian Gugerty, DNS, MS, RN
Bonnie Kaplan, PhD,
Gail Keenan, PhD, RN
Jonathan Leviss, MD
Larry Ozeran, MD
Eric Rose, MD
Scot Silverstein, MD

AHIMA
PRESS

AMIA American Medical
Informatics Association
The professional home for biomedical and health informatics

ISBN 978-1-58426-240-4

AHIMA Product No. AB102209

AHIMA Staff:
Claire Blondeau, MBA, Senior Editor
Cynthia Douglas, Developmental Editor
Katie Greenock, Editorial/Production Editor
Ashley Sullivan, Assistant Editor
Angela K. Dinh, MHA, RHIA, Reviewer
Ken Zielske, Director of Publications

All information contained within this book, including Web sites and regulatory information, was current and valid as of the date of publication. However, Web page addresses and the information on them may change or disappear at any time and for any number of reasons. The user is encouraged to perform his or her own general Web searches to locate any site addresses listed here that are no longer valid.

AHIMA strives to recognize the value of people from every racial and ethnic background as well as all genders, age groups, and sexual orientations by building its membership and leadership resources to reflect the rich diversity of the American population. AHIMA encourages the celebration and promotion of human diversity through education, mentoring, recognition, leadership, and other programs.

American Health Information Management Association
233 North Michigan Avenue, 21st Floor
Chicago, Illinois 60601-5800
http://www.ahima.org

AMIA is the professional home for biomedical and health informatics. AMIA is dedicated to promoting the effective organization, analysis, management, and use of information in health care in support of patient care, public health, teaching, research, administration, and related policy. AMIA's 4,000 members advance the use of health information and communications technology in clinical care and clinical research, personal health management, public health/population, and translational science with the ultimate objective of improving health.

American Medical Informatics Association
4915 St. Elmo Avenue, Suite 401
Bethesda, MD 20814
http://www.amia.org

*To Rebecca and Emily—take chances often,
learn from your failures, and celebrate your successes;
and to Perri (for everything).*

Contents

Contents

IV Appendixes

About the Editors and Contributors

Volume Editor

Jonathan Leviss, MD
Vice President, Chief Medical Officer
Sentillion, Inc.
40 Shattuck Road, Andover, MA 01810
jonathan.leviss@sentillion.com
Staff Physician
Thundermist Health Center, West Warwick, RI

Jonathan Leviss is the Vice President, Chief Medical Officer at Sentillion, Inc., and a staff physician at the Thundermist Health Center in Rhode Island. Dr. Leviss leverages his 15+ years of experience using advanced technologies, including CPOE and EHR systems, to provide medical informatics and healthcare expertise for Sentillion and its customers in the US, Canada, and Europe. He has led many healthcare technology initiatives across inpatient, ambulatory, and community settings and served as the first Chief Medical Informatics Officer at the New York City Health and Hospitals Corporation. Dr. Leviss consulted for academic health systems planning and implementing enterprise-wide health information systems at Deloitte Consulting and at Cerner Corporation. Dr. Leviss is a frequent author and presenter on the subject of medical informatics and has held faculty positions in the departments of medicine at the NYU School of Medicine and the Columbia University College of Physicians and Surgeons. As a practicing primary care physician, Dr. Leviss advises Thundermist Health Center on its EHR rollout and serves as a member of the Rhode Island Clinical Technology Leadership Committee, developing strategies for physician adoption of technology across the state. Dr. Leviss graduated from the NYU School of Medicine and from Tufts University (with a bachelor of arts degree in international relations).

Associate Editors

Brian Gugerty, DNS, MS, RN

Gugerty Consulting, LLC
1038 Bayberry Drive, Arnold, MD 21012
brian_gugerty@hotmail.com

Brian Gugerty has been in the clinical informatics field for 20+ years. Dr. Gugerty is an independent consultant in clinical informatics specializing in EHR implementation and change management. He is also principal consultant to the AMIA endorsed Digital Patient Record Certification Program, the end-user certification for safe and effective use of the digital patient record. Dr. Gugerty taught graduate courses and conducted evaluation research on clinical information systems at the University of Maryland, as an assistant professor where he is now an adjunct professor. He has held positions as Director of Nursing Informatics at a medical center as well as Clinical Information System Product Manager and Senior Research Analyst for leading HIT vendors. He is active in the American Medical Informatics Association as well as other professional societies and initiatives. Dr. Gugerty has published widely and presented on informatics topics including healthcare IT project management, evaluation of healthcare information systems, and informatics education issues.

Bonnie Kaplan, PhD, FACMI

President, Kaplan Associates
33 Ingram Street, Hamden, CT 06517
bonnie.kaplan@yale.edu

Bonnie Kaplan chairs both the American Medical Informatics Association (AMIA) People and Organizational Issues Working Group and the AMIA Ethical, Legal, and Social Issues Working Group and is a fellow of the American College of Medical Informatics. She is President of Kaplan Associates and holds faculty positions as Lecturer at the Yale Center for Medical Informatics and as Adjunct Clinical Professor, Biomedical and Health Information Sciences, University of Illinois – Chicago. She teaches sociotechnical issues and evaluation in the AMIA 10x10 professional certificate program. With more than 35 years of experience in healthcare informatics, Dr. Kaplan led the first workshop

About the Editors and Contributors

at AMIA on health IT project failure. Her consulting and research involves people's reactions to new technologies in healthcare and evaluating applications of computer information systems. She specializes in change management, benefits realization, and identifying and addressing clinician and patient concerns. She also addresses related social and ethical issues concerning new technologies. In 2000 she received the AMIA President's Award for her research and contributions.

Gail Keenan, PhD, RN

Associate Professor
University of Illinois-Chicago
Nursing
845 South Damen Avenue
MC 802, 9th Floor, Chicago, IL 60612
gmkeenan@uic.edu

Gail Keenan is the chair of the AMIA Clinical Information Systems Working Group, the Director of the Nursing Informatics Initiative at the University of Illinois – Chicago, and Chairman and Chief Executive Officer of HealthTeam IQ LLC. Her academic career over the last 10 years has focused on education and research around building and implementing EHRs that support safe and effective communication across the interdisciplinary team. Since 1996, she has served as the principal investigator and leader of a research project that developed, tested, and refined an EHR compatible care planning, "big picture" method called HANDS that enables better handoffs and the generation of comparable data. A 3-year multisite AHRQ funded study of HANDS served as the impetus for making the method available through HealthTeam IQ.

Larry Ozeran, MD

President, Clinical Informatics, Inc.
Suite C
1002 Live Oak Boulevard, Yuba City, CA 95991
doc@drozeran.com

Larry Ozeran has spent 30 years as a computer programmer and database designer and administrator, successfully creating an inpatient EHR with connectivity to legacy systems 20 years ago. Dr. Ozeran has practiced as a general surgeon in rural California since 1992, both in a multispecialty medical group and in solo practice. He has maintained a part-time practice since 2000, at which time he became the President of Clinical Informatics, Inc. Dr. Ozeran also serves as Chair of the Yuba-Sutter Healthcare Council, a broadly representative regional health industry consortium in the early phases of health information collaboration. He has been a vocal proponent of Health Information Technology at the California Medical Association (CMA) since 1996 and actively involved in health policy since 1994, giving many media presentations on health-care reform.

In 2008, Dr. Ozeran was President of the Yuba-Sutter-Colusa Medical Society for a third term. He was selected by county society Presidents throughout California to be the Chair of the CMA Presidents' Forum for the 2008-2009 term. Dr. Ozeran has played a key role in the development of the California eHealth Collaborative, founded in 2009 to promote effective, safe and affordable health information exchange across California. Dr. Ozeran has co-hosted an annual panel on HIT failures at the TEPR (Towards the Electronic Patient Record) conference since 1999. Also, he is a member of the Volunteer Clinical Faculty for the Health Informatics Program at the University California, Davis with an emphasis on politics and policy.

Eric Rose, MD, FAAFP

EHR Product Manager, McKesson Provider Technologies
Clinical Assistant Professor, Department of Family Medicine and Division of Biomedical and Health Informatics,
University of Washington
2210 3rd Avenue West, Seattle, WA 98119
erose@PMSI.com

Eric Rose is a practicing family physician and the medical director at McKesson Provider Technologies. He previously served as the physician informaticist on an ambulatory EHR project at an academic medical center, providing clinical leadership on the first large EHR implementation in the Puget Sound area. Dr. Rose was also a founding work group member of the Certification Commission for Health Information Technology, and continues to serve as co-chair of that organization's Ambulatory Work Group. Dr. Rose holds the position of Clinical Assistant Professor of the Division of Biomedical and Health Informatics and the Department of Family Medicine at the University of Washington School of Medicine, and has been elected Fellow of the American Academy of Family Physicians.

Scot Silverstein, MD

Assistant Professor of Healthcare Informatics and IT
Director, Institute for Healthcare Informatics
College of Information Science and Technology
(Coappointments, School of Public Health, and College of Nursing and Health Profession) Drexel University
3141 Chestnut Street, Philadelphia, PA 19104-2875
scot.silverstein@cis.drexel.edu

Scot Silverstein has more than 15 years of dedicated informatics experience, including management of 50+ employees and budgets of $13 million in academic and industry settings including Yale School of Medicine, Drexel University and Merck & Co., Inc. His work has included informatics projects such as electronic medical records development, customization, and deployment, and clinical data initiatives and registry development. He has expertise in analysis, refinement and reengineering of information-seeking activities and tools, analytic processes, and workflows in biomedical research and clinical care delivery.

Contributing Authors

The editors and publishers would like to thank the following people for contributing the original case studies included in this book. Following is an alphabetical listing of the authors (and author teams).

- Jeffrey M. Adams, PhD(c), RN; Audrey Parks, MBA; and Virginia I. Williams, MSN, RN (coauthors)
- Lawrence B. Afrin, MD; Frank Clark, PhD; John Waller, MD, Patrick Cawley, MD; Timothy Hartzog, MD; Mark Daniels, MS; and Deborah Campbell, RN (coauthors)
- Brian Gugerty, DNS, MS, RN
- Melinda Jenkins, PhD, FNP
- Bonnie Kaplan, PhD
- Gail Keenan, PhD, RN

- Christoph Lehmann, MD; Roberto A. Romero, BS; and George R. Kim, MD (coauthors)
- Jonathan Leviss, MD
- Sandi Mitchell, BS Pharm, MSIS
- Kenneth Ong, MD, MPH
- Larry Ozeran, MD
- Patrick A. Palmieri, EdS, MBA, MSN, ACNP, RN
- Eric Rose, MD
- Scott Silverstein, MD
- Walton Sumner, MD and Phil Asaro, MD
- Vivian Vimarlund, Bahlol Rahimi, and Toomas Timpka (coauthors)
- Riikka Vuokko, Anne Forsell, and Helena Karsten (coauthors)

Cover Illustrations

Morgan DiPietro is a graphic design student at the Maine College of Art located in Portland, ME. Ms. DiPietro discovered her passion for the arts through mural painting and working with local arts organizations as an AmeriCorps*VISTA volunteer in Providence, RI. She also

Acknowledgments

received a BS in Business Communication and Marketing from Bentley University. A selection of her work can viewed at www.morgan-mcallister .blogspot.com.

Additional thanks to Austin Ohm for the idea of a target with darts.

This book exists because of the team effort of the editors, the support of the AMIA Clinical Information Systems Working Group, the information sharing with our colleagues about many, failed—and successful—HIT initiatives, and the professional guidance, editing, and commitment of the AHIMA publishing team.

Introduction and Methodology

Introduction

(J. Leviss, MD, and L. Ozeran, MD)

On February 24, 2009, President Barack Obama pledged to the entire United States Congress, "Our...plan will invest in electronic health records and new technology that will reduce errors, bring down costs, ensure privacy, and save lives" (Obama 2009).

The history of healthcare in the United States, and possibly the world, may one day regard the election of President Barack Obama and the American Recovery and Reinvestment Act of 2009 (ARRA) as a critical inflection point. With the ARRA, President Obama has declared that digitizing healthcare will be a critical success factor in improving healthcare in the US and the overall US economy and has offered large-scale federal funding to create a technology foundation for the US healthcare delivery system. The editors of this book have led successful EHR and HIT projects that brought readily available patient information to all points of healthcare delivery and we are both excited and concered by the potential outcomes of the ARRA funding. Although the ARRA addresses the financial burden of HIT investments, many other challenges remain for successful HIT projects. Some cases to consider:

A hospitalized patient's INR (blood clotting time) becomes dangerously elevated; an investigation finds that the patient received double doses of anticoagulant medication due to an error in how the medication order was processed by the pharmacy computer system after being entered by the CPOE (computerized provider order entry) system. (Chapter 5)

A fire alarm failure in the data center of a tertiary care academic medical center shuts down the hospital information systems. Providers have no access to patient information, including laboratory tests and other results for several hours. (Chapter 4)

A hospital system embarks on an enterprise EHR implementation at great effort and expense, replacing a physician portal; when physicians discover that the new software lacks key functionality available in the old portal, the hospital reimplements the old physician portal. (Chapter 9)

A small physician practice implements an EHR, but even after several years of use, physicians prescribe medications by hand and do not use the EHR to track disease outcomes or to provide reminders about preventive care. (Chapter 16)

> **Health Information Technology (HIT) Failure:** (definition) an HIT failure is one in which an unintended negative consequence occurred, such as a project delay, a substantial cost overrun, a failure to meet an intended goal or objective, or complete abandonment of the project.

HIT projects fail at a rate up to 70% of the time (the sources in the bibliography provide multiple references to such high failure rates); the content and human factors associated with implementing technology have proven to be formidable barriers impeding the widely available transformation that HIT would bring. Moreover, the same lessons or *'best practices'* are being repeatedly learned through trial and error, over and over again, in large and small health systems without successful dissemination of the knowledge among organizations and at great financial cost. Professional conferences routinely share experiences from successful HIT initiatives, but the lessons do not appear to follow the new technologies or update over time; the common errors remain common. As a result, the adoption of effective HIT remains at a fairly primitive stage compared with IT adoption in every other major industry. In fact, healthcare is the **only** trillion dollar industry that remains primarily in the paper stage, even though most healthcare data are available electronically.

The innumerable conferences, webinars, presentations, and publications about HIT success stories have not effectively shared HIT procedural expertise. This collection of HIT case studies offers expert insight into key remaining obstacles that must be overcome to leverage IT in order to modernize and transform healthcare. The purpose of reporting HIT case studies that failed is to document, catalogue, and share key lessons that all project managers of HIT, health system leaders in informatics and technology, hospital executives, policy makers, and service and technology providers must know in order to succeed with HIT, a critical step for the transformation of all health systems.

H.I.T. or Miss presents a model to discuss HIT failures in a *safe and protected manner*, providing an opportunity to focus on the lessons offered by a failed initiative as opposed to worrying about potential retribution for exposing a project as having failed.

At the American Medical Informatics Association (AMIA) 2006 Fall Conference, the Clinical Information Systems Working Group (CIS-WG) hosted an 'open-microphone' event called "Tales from the Trenches" where members shared HIT failure tales from their own institutions. The "Tales From the Trenches" event, created for both professional development and entertainment purposes, quickly proved the value of sharing failure cases and lessons learned in a safe and protected environment. The CIS-WG of AMIA includes a diverse group of individuals with broad experience in HIT. The editors of this book, most of whom were leaders of the CIS-WG, observed a need for a published collection of brief vignettes which documented situations that just didn't go quite right, but could be generalized so a larger audience would learn from the collective wisdom of these stories rather than repeat the same (often costly) mistakes. A call for submissions was distributed across the AMIA CIS-WG listserv (see "Methodology"), resulting in the collection of cases in this book. The editors committed to deidentifying all aspects of the submissions prior to publication and all submitting authors agreed to have their names appear in the book, separate and not linked to their case submissions. The unanimous agreement among all contributing authors to have their names listed in the book reinforces the message that reviewing failed initiatives offers valuable knowledge and insight, rather than an opportunity for casting blame and defensive posturing.

You will find these case studies catalogued by HIT project (for example, CPOE, Ambulatory EHR), but the index will also allow you to search based upon types of lessons learned (for example, project management, technology failure). This approach should enable you, the reader, to find the right anecdote to present to others in your organization that best applies to your specific circumstance.

Learning from failures is an iterative process. Don't permit all of the cost of failure to be borne by your organization. Instead, reflect on these failures as if they occurred in your circumstance so that you can improve your organization's chances of success and reduce your risk of financial loss.

Please feel free to send us your own anecdotes or questions. Even after we have 100% adoption of effective HIT, there will be someone somewhere who needs more information; technologies continually evolve and new information will always be required for their effective (or *meaningful*) use. Maybe that information will come from you. We trust that you will find this collection to be a useful guide along your path.

Methodology

The editorial team for the book, most of whom were part of the AMIA Clinical Information Systems Working Group leadership board, experimented with different case study and analysis lengths, formats, and presentation styles. Ultimately, our experience led to the deidentified model for all names, locations, and other identifying features of a health system or relevant technology, the listing of contributing authors separate from their submitted cases, and the format presented in the book of *Case Study, Author's Analysis,* and *Editor's Commentary.* The purpose of deidentification was to reduce the concern of organizations or individuals reacting negatively to a report of a project's failure to which they were connected, while still permitting lessons to be learned from the failed project. The *Editor's Commentary* provides a second, slightly removed, assessment for additional insight from an informatics expert.

In order to solicit HIT failure cases, the following request was distributed across several AMIA working group listservs and was forwarded to relevant listservs for other organizations:

Submission Instructions

Please submit your story…[to i]nclude the following:

- the title of your HIT failure story: (Definition: an HIT project failure is one in which an unintended negative consequence occurred such as project delays, substantial cost overruns, failure to meet an intended goal or objective, or abandonment of the project)

- a 400-800 word description of the failure, anonymizing the details or using pseudonyms for your characters and organizations

- a 200-400 word discussion of the major lessons you and others learned from the failure

- a statement of whether you want your name included or not included in the book's list of contributing authors

Selection and Publication

All submissions will be carefully reviewed by our editorial team and will be kept confidential. The team will then select...stories to be included in the book and take responsibility for organizing, editing, and providing additional commentary. The author of each selected submission will be asked to sign a statement of originality (attesting that the work has not been previously published) and will receive a free copy of the book once published. All submitting authors' names will be listed separately from the case studies (or not listed at all if preferred), to ensure anonymity. The book will be jointly published by AMIA and at least one other healthcare professional society. All submissions will be kept confidential.

All submissions were reviewed and graded by at least two members of the editorial team for worthiness of inclusion. In cases of discrepancy of reviewers, the Editor reviewed the submission and made a final determination on whether or not the case should be included. In one situation, two case studies described a similar instance in the same institution and the author(s) agreed to allow the editorial team to combine the submissions and author analyses into one case report.

The final step was a review and discussion of the case by a member, or members, of the editorial team. When appropriate, contributing authors and editors included reference material.

The analysis by the editors is purely the opinion of these individuals and does not necessarily reflect the professional opinions of the other editors of the book, AMIA or AHIMA.

Part I

Hospital Care Focus

Chapter 1

Build It with Them, Make It Mandatory, and They Will Come

Implementing CPOE

Editor: B. Kaplan, PhD

Key Words: change management, computerized provider order entry (CPOE), go-live support, pilot

Project Categories: computerized provider order entry (CPOE), inpatient electronic health record (EHR)

Lessons Learned Categories: implementation approaches, leadership

Case Study

Middle Health System has a 650-bed "downtown" hospital, a 350-bed suburban hospital, a 160-bed rehabilitation hospital, and two rural hospitals with 75 to 100 beds. They have 20 other divisions, including a 100-provider medical practice and a visiting nurse business.

Over 15 years, Middle had steady improvements in automation of many business and clinical processes, and then entered another phase, the "clinician high impact" phase of health information technology (HIT). They would acquire and implement new modules of their main vendor's electronic health record (EHR) in their inpatient settings: computerized provider order entry (CPOE), bar code medication administration (BCMA), advanced nursing documentation, and then physician clinical documentation. This would take physicians from occasional users of HIT to dependence on HIT to plan, order, document, and make clinical decisions. The new system would take nurses from moderate users of HIT to heavy users.

CPOE was the first module in the "clinician high impact" phase to be implemented. Middle's chief medical informatics officer position was vacant, so the HIT project came under the direction of the chief information officer (CIO). He was aware of two common recommendations of those who have implemented CPOE:

- "Make CPOE use mandatory."
- "Implement CPOE throughout the enterprise."

However, the CIO thought that mandating use of CPOE was "all well and good for university medical centers," where the ratio of residents to physicians is high. Residents are younger and thus more comfortable with computers; in addition, they are under the direction of their superiors and can be ordered to perform certain tasks. His organization had 50 residents and 1,000 hospitalists, surgeons, midlevel providers, and community doctors. It was unrealistic, he thought, to mandate CPOE. His thinking was: "Build it right, and they will come."

The CPOE planning team also decided on a pilot approach. To mitigate the risk of confusion with a combination of paper and electronic orders, the two nursing units in the suburban hospital that had the fewest transfers from or into other units were chosen as the pilot units.

Despite adequate training of providers and more than adequate support during go-live, several physicians avoided using CPOE on the pilot units from the start. These physicians phoned in their orders so as not to be "harassed" by the bevy of CPOE go-live support staff. Most providers at least tolerated the system but many of those complained of the increased time it took to write orders. Several physicians on the pilot units confided to project team members that they were just "playing along" with the CPOE and were not truly supportive of the change. "If it fails, it will go away, so I don't need to learn it," said one physician who continued to write orders with a pen.

At day 16, 66% of the orders were created via CPOE. A successful pilot was declared. Several of the key players on the CPOE team took vacations. The project manager took 2 weeks off. Upon her return, she discovered that only 15% of the orders were being placed by CPOE. Out of concern for patient safety issues in a mixed CPOE and paper order environment, CPOE was discontinued on the pilot units 2 weeks later.

Author's Analysis

Following are the key lessons learned from the Middle Health System case.

- *Change management is at least as important as technical management, process transformation, and other critical aspects of a CPOE project.* Many people resist change in general. Most clinicians really resist change to their core processes to plan, order, and document care, which a CPOE implementation directly affects. A strong change management plan should be created and executed for a CPOE project.

- *Make CPOE use mandatory for all providers who write orders.* To keep providers from getting around this requirement, have all orders that are not entered directly by CPOE go through a pre-determined process, such as the Joint Commission telephone order read-back procedure: A nurse logs onto the system, retrieves information for the patient in question, enters the order the provider wants, and reads it back to the provider. Because this process takes at least twice as long as the provider ordering directly into the computer via CPOE, providers quickly learn to enter their own orders.

- *Don't call it a "pilot." Consider using a rapid multiphase implementation of CPOE.* Many of the physicians involved regarded the pilot as a tryout of CPOE rather than the beginning of CPOE. You want to give the strong message that phase 1 of implementation is where users learn and then apply the lessons to other units, after a period of consolidation. Through dialogue with clinicians throughout the planning and implementation phases, clear understanding of the benefits and costs of CPOE to not only the organization but to individual organizational members should develop so that people are thinking and saying: "It's here to stay, so I'd better learn it."

- *Don't withdraw CPOE go-live support too quickly.* A user is comfortable after entering orders on approximately 30 patients. A high-volume order writer might write orders on 15 patients per week and thus will have reached the first plateau of competent use of CPOE in about 2 weeks. A low-volume order writer might write orders on one or two patients a week. You may have to keep some scaled-down go-live support for up to 6 months for low-volume order writers.

Editor's Commentary (B. Kaplan, PhD)

It is not unusual for initial enthusiasm or usage to taper off. Two weeks is too short a time for a change to become institutionalized. Many problems can occur in the first few weeks without warranting discontinuing an implementation, and apparent successes can occur without warranting that all is well. Sustained support, reinforcement, and evaluating what is happening are needed to maintain a desired trajectory.

Attention should have been paid to early indicators that there could be problems. Not all providers were willing to use the system so as to avoid what they considered "harassment" by the support staff. Others "at least tolerated the system" but complained that it took longer to write orders. Some even confided that they were not supportive of the change, but were "playing along." None of these issues was addressed. If it would take longer to enter orders, physicians would need to understand why CPOE was important. Perhaps the time it takes to enter orders would decrease as staff learned better how to use the system, in which case they should have been helped both to understand the learning curve and to grasp concepts more quickly. Training, however, was described as "at least adequate" when it could have been better than minimally sufficient.

Different user communities, such as nurses and physicians, will have different incentives, training and support needs, attitudes, and aptitudes that need addressing. The benefits of using the system, or at least reasons why it should be used even if there are no obvious benefits to the users, also need to be highlighted and reinforced.

The pilot units were chosen because they had a low volume of transfers. The case study does not indicate how these units were viewed by the rest of the organization or whether there were other characteristics that could have affected what developed. A positive experience with the first units where change is implemented will serve as a good example to other units. In addition to selecting a test bed that is not too challenging, as was done here, other considerations include whether people on the unit might be respected project champions and if there is strong leadership support in the unit for the project.

Another issue is that several key players took vacation at the same time, which was very early in the implementation. Although the vacation time was likely well deserved, having several key players gone at the same time meant there were not enough people available to notice and address the developing problem of nonuse of CPOE. Mechanisms to assess progress and take steps to alleviate problematic developments before they got out of hand should have been in place. Especially in the early days of implementation, it can be quite helpful to continue with training efforts as unfamiliar situations are encountered, and also to monitor where things do not go smoothly, where workarounds are occurring, and where complaints are developing. It appears there was no such plan in place, and without key people on site, there was no ad hoc means of addressing emerging issues. As a result, an early success quickly turned into an early failure.

Lessons Learned

- Change management is critical for CPOE projects
- Make CPOE mandatory
- Don't call it a "pilot"
- Don't withdraw CPOE go-live support too quickly

Chapter 2

Hospital Objectives vs. Project Timelines

An Electronic Medication Administration Record (eMAR)

Editor: B. Gugerty, DNS, MS, RN

Key Words: clinical information system, clinician leadership, help desk, medication administration, stakeholder input, workstations on wheels (WOWs)

Project Categories: electronic medication administration record (eMAR), inpatient electronic health record (EHR)

Lessons Learned Categories: communication, leadership, staffing resources, technology problems

Case Study

The chief information officer (CIO) at a large teaching hospital, with support from executive management at the hospital, committed to implementing an electronic medication administration record (eMAR) with bedside documentation. The project was to be featured in the hospital's Joint Commission accreditation inspection during the next year. The CIO highlighted the risks inherent in paper MARs including the limited ability for a nurse to have up-to-date information from a patient's paper medication list. A medicine teaching service was selected for the pilot. The hospital had already implemented broad functionality with a robust clinical information system, but the eMAR represented the first initiative that required 100% compliance by clinicians for clinical data entry, rather than the optional computerized provider order entry (CPOE) and clinical documentation modules, diagnostic test results system, and picture archiving communication system (PACS) implemented previously. Several dependencies were identified during the early planning stages for the project:

- Extensive development of an integrated medication management system by the core healthcare information system (HIS) vendor, including new functionality for CPOE, pharmacy medication management, and the eMAR
- Workflow transformation for nurses, pharmacists, and physicians in the medication management process (from order entry by physicians, through order verification and medication preparation by pharmacists, to medication administration and patient assessment by nurses)
- New hardware procurement and installation to support the new eMAR, including a wireless network in the pilot inpatient unit
- Software configuration by the hospital information technology (IT) team and the vendor
- Implementation of the new software
- Training of all involved staff

The vendor worked with an interdisciplinary team of IT staff, nurses, pharmacists, and physicians to develop the functionality necessary to support best practices for medication management, from ordering to administration. Various committees met monthly, weekly, and even daily, with participants numbering from 2 to 40 depending on the topic addressed. The collective input and collaboration enabled the group to explore new concepts of interdisciplinary medication management, including pharmacy-physician communication for medication dose adjustment and confidential reporting of adverse drug events and medication errors.

Vendors demonstrated WOWs of different sizes, weights, and with varying degrees of mobility, to the nursing and IT groups. The interdisciplinary group evaluated different laptops, recognizing that size, weight, ease of use, and even battery life would be important to the success of the eMAR. Best practices in system design and implementation appeared to be in place for the important patient safety initiative; the hospital continually stressed the importance of the project for the Joint Commission visit.

Project timelines began to slip. With only a few months before the scheduled go-live, the vendor delayed the delivery of the software. Additionally, the hospital's help desk became overburdened with support issues for existing systems, including problems of access to clinical systems, certain functions of the HIS, and properly functioning printers, computers, and monitors. In the final month before go-live, the mobile computer vendor announced a delay in the delivery of the WOWs for the pilot.

Several clinician leaders requested that the project wait until all systems could be fully tested and until the hospital refocused on routine operations after the scheduled Joint Commission visit, but the CIO remained committed to completing the initiative because it was to be a highlight in the Joint Commission visit. Ultimately, all devices arrived on the eMAR pilot medicine inpatient unit; the IT team implemented the software; and the nursing unit went live. For several days, the IT team staffed the pilot unit around the clock with nurses trained in the new eMAR to assist physicians, pharmacists, and nurses with the rollout. Clinical and administrative staff reacted well to the rollout, and the Joint Commission inspection team noted the achievement as evidence of leadership in the field of healthcare technology. Then, the focus on the pilot unit faded.

Over the next few weeks, several changes occurred on the pilot unit. The nurses who regularly staffed the unit, and whose average age was about 10 years older than those who selected the WOWs for the eMAR, complained of difficulty reading the small fonts on the screens of the WOWs. Nurses who rotated to the medicine unit after the heavily staffed rollout said they received inadequate training on the eMAR and preferred the previous paper MAR. The WOWs began crashing and freezing during regular use, requiring frequent reboots; nurses found that leaving the devices standing in the nursing station prevented such dysfunction but also prevented bedside use of the technology. Calls to the IT help desk for support went unanswered for up to 72 hours. Meanwhile, the CIO continued to discuss the successful pilot, unaware that nurses on the pilot unit had begun to print out a paper MAR for use on each shift; the paper MAR could be brought to the patient's bedside. The nurses relied on the paper MAR for patient care, updating changes in the patient's record at the end of the shift, just as they did prior to the rollout of the eMAR. During follow-up interviews at the pilot site, the nurses on the unit were surprised to learn that corporate management

I could not agree more with the author's statement that "most importantly, clinical IT initiatives require the leadership of the clinician end-users" if by leadership it is not understood that the clinician end-user literally has to be leading the project. Perhaps the widely used (outside of the U.S., anyway) PRINCE2 project management methodology (Office of Government Commerce 2009), where the project manager reports to a project board composed of an executive sponsor from the organization, a senior representative of the end-user community, and a senior technical representative throughout the entire project, could allow effective clinical end-user leadership. The glaring leadership failure in this case study, in my mind at least, was with the CIO focusing on the achievement of his or her apparent real goal of creating "evidence of leadership in the field of healthcare technology" at the expense of solidifying carefully crafted new processes that improved patient safety.

Lessons Learned

- Clinician leadership is critical to HIT initiatives
- IT support is critical during, and just after, a go-live
- Effective project planning includes proper resource management

Chapter 3

Clinical Quality Improvement or Administrative Oversight

Clinical Decision Support Systems

Editor: J. Leviss, MD

Key Words: clinical decision support, clinical guidelines, data quality, quality assurance, workflow

Project Categories: computerized provider order entry (CPOE), inpatient electronic health record (EHR)

Lessons Learned Categories: communication, workflow

Case Study

Hospital administration was proud because clinicians at their small hospital were using a new clinical decision support system that alerted them when standard clinical practices were not followed. The system checked laboratory and medication orders against diagnoses in one specialty area, matched those diagnoses with symptoms for conditions, and also issued alerts when various data indicated abnormalities. The new system, the administration was convinced, was improving quality. It worked so well that they wanted to extend its use from inpatient to ambulatory care.

Direct observations and questions of end-users raised additional questions, however. Some attending physicians said the system was good, but was mainly for less skilled clinicians or for residents who still needed to learn. Those residents and clinicians said it was good for reviewing diagnostic criteria and guidelines, but the alerts did not really provide new information or result in changed orders or practice. Further, in order to get past the requirement that all required symptoms had to be entered before the diagnosis would be accepted by the software, residents entered the symptoms they knew to be required, not necessarily the symptoms the patient had. The head of resident training knew there were problems, but also wanted to support Administration.

Administration had tried to do everything right. They used a participatory design approach and the head of quality assurance, himself a physician, was a key figure in the project. A local computer scientist had produced the system in close consultation with clinical and quality assurance staff. All clinicians were trained to use the system, as were residents when they began their rotations at this hospital.

Clinical staff, however, did not feel involved in creating the system or in determining when and how it was used. Clinicians saw the system as the administration's reporting tool, whereas the administration described the system as benefiting clinicians and improving clinical care. Further, the clinical staff felt pressured, recently having gone through a merger with a nearby larger hospital and having to adjust to new ways of doing things. For them, the clinical decision support system was yet another burden.

Even with the problems, the system did report mismatches between symptoms and diagnosis, diagnosis and orders for medications or laboratory work, and alerts for abnormalities. The use of this system was well in advance of other hospitals, and the administration was proud of the progress made. They did not know about the underlying issues, but had wisely brought in others to investigate before rolling out the system for outpatient care. Administration and the clinicians had different notions of success.

Author's Analysis

Lesson 1: Watch what people do rather than depend only on what they say. The ways residents were gaming the system were not apparent until outside consultants observed residents showing each other how to enter data from a new patient into the system, explaining ways to circumvent some of the system's controls. Of course, it was not presented quite that starkly, but almost.

Lesson 2: Pay attention to data quality and to the influencing factors. Quality assurance was based on the data entered by the clinicians. Quality assurance staff thought that data entered by clinicians improved care, as documented by reports derived from these data. Clinicians, though, were sometimes entering data that reflected their understanding of system requirements rather than their examination of the patient, even when they knew the two might be in conflict. Consider trustworthiness of data in light of system requirements and reward structures.

Lesson 3: Incorporation of practice guidelines into clinical decision support systems does not necessarily result in increased compliance with the guidelines if workarounds and "system gaming" occur.

Lesson 4: There always will be problems. The trick is to identify the problems before they cause harm. Evaluation is necessary and should be done in skillful and nonthreatening ways that can uncover what is happening on the floors, in treatment areas, in residents' rooms—anywhere HIT is used, or supposed to be used. Often evaluation needs to be independent—either independent from the project team or the health system.

Editor's Commentary (J. Leviss, MD)

The case study highlights three key lessons: integrating effective clinical decision support is challenging; clinicians are people–they work in health systems and are affected by the current issues and culture of their organization; projects require effective ongoing evaluation.

The wealth of literature on failed and successful computerized decision support documents the difficulties in introducing the right knowledge to physicians at the right point in care delivery without creating burdensome work or providing information that is already known or irrelevant to a particular patient. Additional references discussing this topic are included at the end of this case discussion.

Introducing information systems to clinical care requires changing the way clinicians interact with patients and gather and process information *and* challenges their decision-making at the point of care in front of both colleagues and patients. These changes can be stressful for clinicians; if other major stressors already exist, such as a recent hospital merger, new programs to measure clinicians' quality performance, or decreased physician income, then the stress of a new HIT system may be impossible to bear. Organizations need to recognize the stress level and tolerance for change of their own staffs and plan accordingly so that successful initiatives can be introduced at appropriate times. A delayed project that succeeds is more valuable, and less expensive, than a project started on time that fails.

Objective evaluation is critical to determine what aspects of a project should be continued, or expanded, and what aspects should be modified. Depending on the size of the project, scope, and complexity, an evaluation could be extensive or brief. Part of ongoing evaluation also requires regular, open communication between the end-user community, the health system management, and the IT project team. Most health systems that succeed in creating the open dialogue between these groups have a system of interdisciplinary informatics governance—models range from interdisciplinary committees to role-based committees with committee chairs joining together in interdisciplinary forums to foster open communication. Both approaches typically involve quality management. The essential component is the opportunity for hospital management, IT, and the clinicians to express their views, concerns, and experiences, while also listening to those of the other groups. Transparent discussions about positive and negative aspects of HIT initiatives help reveal problems early for effective resolution. Sometimes, outside expertise is required to objectively evaluate a project and to remove any positive or negative bias; "outside" could mean simply someone other than the project team members or a contracted consultant with expertise in the area of the project for evaluation. Large health systems could even rotate individuals to facilities other than their primary site of work to serve as evaluators. Evaluation should be part of the improvement cycle of an HIT project, if not throughout the entire project life cycle, providing insight to further improve the initiative.

Lessons Learned

- Expect problems; the key is evaluating projects to identify problems and address them early
- IT quality assurance requires some in-depth review of data, clinician workflow, and other details of a new process and/or technology
- Organizational culture and current circumstances may limit the ability for members to change processes. A culture that inhibits direct and open communication leads to diminished stakeholder input in favor of conflict avoidance behaviors that often defeat the intent of HIT systems.

Additional Reading:

Kuperman, G.J., A. Bobb, T.H. Payne, A.J. Avery, T.K. Gandhi, G. Burns, D.C. Classen, D.W. Bates. 2007. Medication-related clinical decision support in computerized provider order entry systems: A review. *Journal of the American Medical Informatics Association* 14 (1):29-40.

Kuperman, G.J., R.M. Reichley, T.C. Bailey. 2006. *Journal of the American Medical Informatics Association* 13 (4):369-71.

Killelea, B.K., R. Kaushal, M. Cooper, G.J. Kuperman. 2007. To what extent do pediatricians accept computer-based dosing suggestions? *Pediatrics* 119 (1).

CPOE, pharmacy dispensing, admission-discharge-transfer (ADT), and intensive care unit (ICU) clinical documentation.

Example 1

In 2005, a failure of the data center fire alarm system occurred; a piece of plastic within the housing of the wall-mounted fire alarm broke. (The manufacturing cost of the failing piece was less than $1.) This resulted in the triggering of the fire alarm with a subsequent programmed, orderly shutdown of all servers, discontinuation of electric power, and release of the fire suppressant agent Halon into the data center.

For several hours, all data center services were unavailable, and providers had to switch to paper-based ordering and charting until the emergent problem was handled. Once the source of the alarm was identified and the Halon was cleared, the clinical data systems were restarted without data loss and with resumption of normal function.

Example 2

Two years later, a weekend water outage in the building housing the data center was scheduled by the maintenance staff, but was not properly communicated to the engineering staff. Despite a clearly posted policy to the contrary, maintenance staff disabled a primary water pump supplying water to the building.

The water outage interrupted the chilled water supply to the data center air handlers and resulted in a malfunction, which in turn shut down the air conditioning in the building. This resulted in a rise in environmental temperature that was detected by sensors, resulting in a programmed shutdown of the clinical servers, followed by discontinuation of electric power to the data center. Because the smoke alarm was not triggered, the fire suppression agent was not released.

Data center personnel were notified immediately of the shutdown, but its cause (air conditioning failure due to the water outage) was not immediately apparent. After several hours, water services were restored, the air conditioning was restarted, and the temperature in the data center was normalized. The clinical data systems servers were restarted without data loss.

The water outage (and the resulting cascade of air conditioning failure and data center outage) forced the clinical staff to revert to paper ordering and charting. The incident resulted in no apparent patient harm, but lack of complete and accurate data was found to be a major user concern when the incident was reviewed by an institutional committee.

Author's Analysis

Closed loop systems (as described in the data center environmental protection system in the previous examples) automate system responses (system shutdown, threat mitigation, and staff alert) to specified rules from defined input (abnormal environmental variables). In high-risk industries such as aeronautics and nuclear power, they are used to aid human operators (who in turn override inappropriate machine responses). In clinical care, they have been used to control experimental insulin pumps, pacemakers, and anesthesia machines, but sparingly, because of inherent risks.

"Who monitors the monitors?" is an apt question regarding the design of closed loop systems in enterprise health information systems. The increasing reliance on clinical information technology system (since the last scenario in 2007, CPOE use within the health system has increased to 80 percent of all physician orders) make unanticipated outages (even short ones), as described in the foregoing examples, highly disruptive to continuity of care and may jeopardize patient care with errors of omission/commission and preventable delays.

Clinical data centers must ensure information (its confidentiality, integrity, and availability) with minimal unplanned downtime. With robust designs, unplanned outages are usually minimal, and closed loop environmental monitors, as described in the examples, usually work well, thus not warranting human surveillance. However, current designs are limited to a few independent data measurements and cannot distinguish between a true threat and an internal monitoring failure. The data center monitoring system was originally implemented with the assumption that shutting down the servers in an emergency is preferable (even in error) to data loss from continued operation resulting in permanent damage. With increasing institutional reliance, the error of commission was becoming increasingly problematic and disruptive.

What can be learned from these outages?

Data centers are "single points of failure" that are protected by monitoring systems that shut down according to a predefined set of rules that have thresholds.

The acceptability of these thresholds may change over time because of changes in institutional dependence on the data center, which may require re-assessment of failure modes and their acceptability.

Planning of protection responses may require consideration of unanticipated "normal" events external to the data center with override rules, workaround protocols, and timely and appropriate human interventions.

In the case of the described institution, a remote redundant secondary data center was built. Clinical systems are now configured to switch to the secondary data center automatically in a 'near real-time' fashion in the event of an outage in the primary center.

Hospital administrators, IT staff, and vendors must be aware of how defense systems for data centers function and how they fail. They also should evolve these systems from experience. The design of redundant systems (backup environmental systems and power sources, alternative short-term data storage), of "smart" closed loop systems that infer the likelihood of true threats based on multiple inputs, and of critical defense protocols are key in maintaining system availability.

Editor's Commentary (B. Kaplan, PhD)

Both of the examples describe unanticipated ways that system failure occurs. Each time, sensors detected abnormalities that led to automatic shutdown of a data center. In the first example, an inexpensive plastic piece in the fire alarm housing broke. This triggered a fire alarm, a shutdown, and firefighting actions, even though there was no fire. In the second example, workers disabled a water pump and did not notify system engineers, despite clear policy to the contrary. The disabled pump caused an air conditioning failure, which then caused the system to shut down as the temperature rose past the cutoff point. In each example, staff reverted to manual medical record keeping with no apparent patient harm. However, staff were concerned about lack of complete and accurate data after the second incident. Because increasing system use would make system outages even more disruptive, a remote redundant secondary data center was established so that system functions would be switched there if an outage occurred at the primary center.

As the author points out, contingency planning and manual procedures are vital. The examples indicate how important it was to have staff able to switch to manual procedures when automated ones failed. Moreover, a wise decision was made when a secondary data center was established so that crucial system functions could be continued smoothly if the primary center fails. Even though problems could again occur at either the primary or secondary center, the likelihood of them occurring simultaneously at both centers is small. Nevertheless, as the examples amply show, all sorts of unanticipated things may happen. The examples also show that failures can occur for many interrelated reasons. As the author rightly says, it is not possible to respond correctly to all situations in systems by monitoring according to predefined rules. Thresholds need to be reevaluated periodically.

I think other potential safeguards also are suggested by these examples. Would it not be better to try reducing such alarms? In the first example, a plastic part broke, and that triggered the fire alarm, causing a several-hour shutdown. It was difficult to identify the cause of the problem. Perhaps routine parts inspections or replacements would have prevented the problem. Perhaps better awareness of vulnerabilities of this sort would have been helpful. Perhaps redundancy, such as noticing the lack of smoke or heat detection, would have helped.

The second example points even more strongly to a variety of interlocking causes and multiple failure points, leading to multiple possibilities for preventive measures. Policy violations meant that staff was not notified of the water outage, and that a crucial pump was disabled. Either workers were ignorant of the policy or disregarded it. Remedial action is needed, but what action should be based on the reason for the policy violations? Workers could be better trained and the policy rationale better explained, or maybe the policy itself needs revision. The policy could be posted more clearly. A sign-off could be instituted when crucial functions are to be interrupted. If various utilities (water, electricity) are interrupted routinely, an alert system might be put in place to warn data center staff.

These are some possible ideas. Others might well make more sense. Without knowing the institution, those involved, and reasons for failure beyond those built into the automatic system, it is hard to make sound recommendations. Instead, the suggestions are meant to illustrate an important point when analyzing problematic situations. There are different ways to analyze causes of failure so as to remediate them. The focus can be on the system itself. Maybe hardware or software is to blame. In these examples, there clearly were system failures caused by automatic built-in responses. Reevaluating thresholds is one way to address this issue, as is having a secondary backup center. Alternatively, the focus can be on personnel. When policies are violated, new procedures and training can be instituted. When systems go down, patient care functions continued with limited loss of patient data or threats to patient safety because staff was well prepared and acted appropriately. Finally, the focus can be on how everything -- system, personnel, and procedures -- works together in interrelated ways that these examples beautifully illustrate. Broadening "system" to include personnel and procedures as well as hardware and software could provide a wider perspective on how to better design safeguards. All three of these perspectives can help address failures.

The title of this chapter shortchanges the richness of these examples. Rather, the stories indicate multiple failure points and ways to address them.

Additional Reading:

Kilbridge, P. 2003. Computer crash: Lessons from a system failure. *N Engl J Med* Mar 6;348(10):881-882.

Lessons Learned

- Downtime management requires complex planning
- System redundancy is required across all components of HIT
- Automated alarms and processes must be appropriate to a specific environment
- System interdependencies cannot be overestimated
- Policies and procedures must include enforcement and training/ re-training
- Communication is crucial

Chapter 5

Basic Math

<hr>

The HL7 Message:
CPOE to Pharmacy to eMAR

Editor: L. Ozeran, MD and J. Leviss, MD

Key Words: computerized provider order entry (CPOE), electronic medication administration record (eMAR), Health Level 7 (HL7) interface, pharmacy, test system

Project Categories: computerized provider order entry (CPOE), electronic medication administration record (eMAR), inpatient electronic health record (EHR)

Lessons Learned Categories: system configuration, technology problem

Case Study

<hr>

In our CPOE system, a medication order was generated for warfarin 7 mg daily. Using an HL7 interface message, the medication order was communicated to an external pharmacy system. Because there is no commercial product of warfarin 7 mg, the pharmacist converted the order into dispensable products, a 5-mg tablet and a 2-mg tablet.

Several days later, clinicians observed that the patient's anticoagulation laboratory results (INR) were at panic levels, but there had been no easily identified originating event. The anticoagulation medications were reviewed and the clinicians were surprised at the warfarin dosing – it was much higher than originally ordered. The clinicians ordered a dose of warfarin 7 mg daily, yet the order and the eMAR both indicated a dose of warfarin 14 mg. Upon review of the audit trail, the provider entered warfarin 7 mg, but after the Pharmacy verification, the order was modified to warfarin 14 mg.

The first step was to implement an immediate workaround, which was to discontinue the order and reenter the medication order differently. Because the medication dose required two separate products to be dispensed (warfarin 2 mg and 5 mg), the order was reentered successfully as two separate medication orders.

Author's Analysis

The complexities of an interfaced medication order between two disparate vendor applications cannot be overestimated. Iatrogenic events can change the data outcome and affect clinical outcomes.

The complexities of HL7 include both the technology standards and the semantic standards. Events like a medication order generate an HL7 message that is communicated through an interface engine and then to the receiving system. As the message travels, each computer has the ability to interpret and even modify the content of the data based on defined algorithms.

During evaluation, the situation was replicated in our test system. The troubleshooting efforts were focused on the multiple product situation. Because the medication dose required two separate products be dispensed, the successful workaround was to enter two separate orders while the troubleshooting continued. In the CPOE system, the medication is ordered as a generic name and a dose, without product level considerations.

Appropriately, within a pharmacy application, the medication order was interpreted into the dispensing product level. Within this pharmacy system, there was functionality for a multiproduct medication order being represented as a single medication order. If the generic formulary item is the same, the medication dose requiring two products can be combined in a single order. The warfarin 7 mg order included two dispensing products – warfarin 2 mg and warfarin 5 mg.

Upon review, the original CPOE HL7 message that was sent to the pharmacy system was passed through an enterprise interface engine and then a CPOE interface engine before being received by the external pharmacy application and used the same route upon return to the CPOE system. The CPOE system identified the generic product and dose while the pharmacy system identified the generic and dispensing products required to provide the dose.

In HL7, the "RXE" segment represents the pharmacy encoded order data (Hann's On Software 2008). The "Give amount" and "Give units" values are updated during the "perfection process" (pharmacy verification). With a multiproduct order, two separate RXE segments are defined. In this case, there were two RXE segments, one for warfarin 2 mg and one for warfarin 5 mg. The unexpected data transformation included the pharmacy application having a process to manage multiple RXE segments. The result was that instead of adding the amounts to a total dose, it multiplied the subcomponents, thus generating 14 mg instead of the expected 7 mg. So the calculation was:

2 RXE components x (2 mg) + 2 RXE components x (5 mg) = 14 mg

The CPOE application accepted the verification with the dose modification from the pharmacy system and changed the order view and the eMAR view of the order to a dose of 14 mg. There was no alert, only an overwriting of the original order; the modification went unnoticed until a clinical situation arose.

Once the issue was identified, additional testing confirmed the situation, and the vendor was contacted. The issue had the highest vendor priority, and a fix was available the next day. On site, reports were generated to check for any other instances of the situation, one additional patient was identified and the clinicians were immediately involved. There were no adverse long-term impacts to either of the patients.

Editor's Commentary (L. Ozeran, MD and J. Leviss, MD)

This scenario reminds us of some very important lessons.

1) *You often don't know what you don't know.*

This is why it is critical to check all of your assumptions when something goes wrong. The authors and their institution must be commended for having a clear process for investigating problems. They planned for failure and how to manage it.

2) *Computers* **DO** *make mistakes, when we provide the wrong information or the wrong instructions.*

There is a tendency to think that the data we get from the computer must be right, simply because it came from the computer. This expectation and the resultant complacency can blind us to embedded errors. One key component of evaluating the information exchanged by systems is thorough testing, such as that performed in a test laboratory similar to that described by the authors; rigorous testing is critical prior to implementing new technologies and even upgrades to existing systems.

What was the testing process prior to this implementation? Testing of closed loop medication systems, for example, should focus on both typical, straightforward orders as well as very complex ones, such as the warfarin order previously described. Although testing may not identify all problems, a broad testing strategy should dramatically decrease the likelihood of errors such as that described earlier. If warfarin orders were being divided automatically, perhaps other similar orders were also affected by the system, such as complex doses of medications or parenteral nutrition. Testing protocols should include these challenging scenarios. Anecdotal evidence indicates that many hospitals do not have appropriately replicated environments in which to thoroughly test systems prior to rollout; test environments may not include the full array of clinical information systems, a sufficiently large test database, or involve clinicians who understand the more sophisticated data flows that are generated during clinical care. The practice of thorough testing should be part of any technology implementation.

3) *Whenever we computerize a medical process to reduce errors, there is always a risk that new errors will be introduced.*

The currently widespread political support for CPOE and ePharmacy is appropriate, but also concerning. Many politicians see only the potential benefits and do not acknowledge or understand the potential risks. The current political and regulatory environment is setting unreasonably glowing expectations for HIT. In many ways, this specific error was caught quickly because there was an easily observable clinical effect that did not kill patients before the culprit could be identified. Had the dosing been for digoxin, a very different outcome might have resulted. In that case, it might have been very difficult to identify a pattern among a few patients because digoxin becomes toxic more slowly. We must remember that every change that can bring an improvement to our provision of healthcare can also bring new problems. We must be diligent about finding those problems. That means that managers, executives, regulators, legislators, and every other leader who plays a role in our healthcare system must be aware that technology brings costs beyond the financial, and they must support implementing technology safely. We must properly balance accuracy with speeding change.

Lessons Learned

- Perform extensive testing with a large number of scenarios involving different product level data
- Involve clinicians who are technology savvy to participate in testing of scenarios
- Empower all clinicians to question medication doses and other aspects of clinical care processes, even if they involve information systems

Chapter 6

Technological Iatrogenesis from "Downtime"

Pharmacy and Medication Systems

Editor: J. Leviss, MD and L. Ozeran, MD

Key Words: adverse event, allergy, computerized provider order entry (CPOE), downtime, medication administration, patient safety, pharmacy, training, vendor contract

Project Categories: electronic medication administration record (eMAR), inpatient electronic health record (EHR), pharmacy IS

Lessons Learned Categories: communication, contracts, leadership, staffing resources, technology problems, training

Case Study

At 4 a.m. I was paged at home by the pharmacy director; I called back to hear, "one of your nurses has really messed up this time…nearly killed a patient."

I arrived at the hospital intensive care unit (ICU) break room to see a capable and experienced nurse sobbing, thinking she was solely responsible for seriously harming a patient. I felt bad—-this nurse had switched from day shifts to nights to help orient several new nurses. After comforting the nurse, I listened to her recollect the events of the incident. At 2 a.m. the nurse went to the automated medication dispensing unit to obtain an antibiotic (AB) for a patient. She selected and retrieved the AB for the patient and then promptly delivered it. Shortly after medication delivery, the patient experienced respiratory arrest.

The nurse explained that the patient had a serious allergy to the AB she administered. Immediately, I assumed that we did not know about the allergy or someone failed to enter the patient's allergy into the medication module in the pharmacy. In any case, I thought the nurse should have checked the arm band, or the chart, and been more careful in the delivery of the scheduled medications. Yes, I thought, she should have adhered to the five rights.

Later that morning, I began to complete the cumbersome paperwork that accompanies adverse events. I found the AB allergy appropriately listed in the patient's pharmacy medication profile. Next, I discovered that the nurse selected a similarly spelled, yet altogether different, medication from that ordered. The case prompted a conversation with the pharmacy director about our medication delivery system. The ICU was scheduled for the "go-live" with bar code medication administration (BCMA) in 3 months. I knew this situation would provide for a lively discussion at the Pharmacy and Therapeutics (P&T) Committee, as the chair believes the new technologies will help nurses stop making errors.

Author's Analysis

After conducting an investigation, followed by a root cause analysis, we found the following issues involved technology:

1. The pharmacy-unit medication cabinet interface for the ICU was inoperable, or "down," at the time of the event.
   a. The hospital required the administrator on call to be immediately notified when a system was "down."

2. The pharmacy was aware the system was down but this appeared to be a normal "update time" from 11 p.m. and 3 a.m.
   a. Paper shift reports showed that the system was down nearly 60% of the time during the hours of 11 p.m. and 3 a.m. (although updates were not regularly occurring)

3. The vendor acknowledged awareness that the system was down, but had not reported the issue to the P&T Committee because a fix was imminent. The vendor did not consider the system "down" because all other interfaces were functional.

4. The on-call hospitalist ordered the new medication for an unfamiliar patient in response to important new blood culture results.
   a. The nurse and physician did not verbally discuss the order.
   b. Follow-up testing could not duplicate the medication order in the CPOE system without an override, even with repeated mock attempts.
5. Nurses at night were used to the system being down, but day nurses rarely experienced this downtime.
   a. The night nurses did not think down time warranted an incident report.
6. The hospital had no policies and procedures to monitor technology quality, such as system reliability.
7. Most importantly, everyone thought that someone else knew about this problem.

The operational failure the nurse unexpectedly discovered was that the medication dispensing machine was unable to profile each patient's medication record. When a patient-specific medication profile was absent, the dispensing machine's entire pharmaceutical contents were readily available and the patient profile (for example, allergies) was not present as a protective layer. Notably, a clinician was able to remove the wrong medication or the wrong medication dose from the dispensing unit, an act that was only possible with an override when the pharmacy-machine interface was properly functioning. Also, the BCMA system would be rendered ineffective when the interface was disrupted, creating the precondition for potentially serious events in the other units.

HIT operational failures may result more often than reported in the literature because of stealth operational failures that only manifest when a patient is seriously harmed and investigation and root cause analysis are conducted. The sociotechnical system is quite complex, and tightly coupled, with the propensity to generate rapid error cascades that end in technological iatrogenesis. In this case, the unanticipated latent failure, "down times," manifested as an active error and sentinel event. When technology and people become disconnected because of "down times" associated with system interfaces, a nontrivial latent failure is immediately present and places the system at risk for failure.

HIT system implementations in hospitals pledge to make patients safer and to provide clinicians with safety supports as they work hard to provide quality care. However, the nurse involved in this event trusted the system and became dependent on the technology without realizing the potential negative consequences. The HIT provided a safety illusion. Also important to note, the trust placed in the vendor to work as a partner was inappropriate. Unfortunately for the patient harmed and the nurse traumatized, the vendor did not function as a partner in safety; commercial contract concerns overrode disclosures. An important lesson learned is that all management safety expectations (reporting, expected outcomes, system reliability) should be reduced to writing as part of the contract.

Editor's Commentary (J. Leviss, MD and L. Ozeran, MD)

The medication error documented in this chapter illustrates key failure points that can occur in an HIT initiative, including:

- Communication—CPOE systems, especially when integrated with pharmacy systems and medication administration systems, eliminate much of the verbal communication between physicians, nurses, pharmacists, and even laboratory technicians or ancillary staff. When HIT systems are implemented, full workflow analyses, including communication practices, should be evaluated to identify what steps are being replaced or changed and what the potential impact might be. Sometimes a valuable check existed in the paper world that might be lost with the new process that was particularly important to a specific unit, team, or organization. Just because it is common for a system to stop functioning does not mean that it is a normal condition. Complacency about the nonfunctional status quo nearly killed a patient.

- System performance—Technology downtime is a critical issue in healthcare, a continuous process which runs 24/7 all year long. Scheduled "down times" require specific policies and processes, just as unscheduled down times. They should be no longer than necessary and policies should clearly outline what clinical staff is to do during those down times to ensure patient safety. Physicians and nurses learn to benefit from medication safety technology and shift the focus to patient management issues not protected by an information system, such as double-checking infusion rates instead of medication name spelling. When the safety support is withdrawn from the first issue, a worse situation could result. Hospitals run disaster drills, and even fire drills, but how many run HIT downtime drills to keep staff aware of down-time processes? Downtime drills keep all staff aware of their role in alerting peers and leadership to problems and the role of incident reports for HIT problems.

- Leadership—Leadership must define performance criteria for an HIT initiative, including the minimal technical performance metrics, and create policies and processes for technical insufficiencies. Projects must be monitored for achieving planned metrics, and policies must be monitored for adherence.

- Staffing/Training—It is common in our high-stress environments where time and resources are at a premium for training to be inadequate. In this case, the nurse on duty had not been adequately trained with regard to the limitations of the system during the night shift and had not been taught what she needed to do in order to ensure patient safety. Although it is commonplace for a new hire to be trained to become familiar with a new institution, it is less common for retraining to occur when an existing employee moves to another part of a facility, or in this case, another shift. Each area should have a standard training process, even if some of it is review for those already working for the organization.

- Contracts—Contracts should clearly state the goals and objectives of the business relationship between a vendor and customer, but contracts are usually invoked when something goes wrong. Project vigilance and transparent communication are the most important components of a successful customer-vendor engagement, like any relationship.

Finally, the author describes an investigation process into an adverse event that should be applied through failure mode analysis before going live with an automated solution. All of these approaches require resources that not all health systems are able to commit, but perhaps should be required to do so.

Lessons Learned

- Communication is crucial among all users and stakeholders, especially when an issue or error arises
- System performance should be monitored continually
- Leadership is essential to maintain focus on project and system goals and objectives
- Staffing/training must be ongoing to ensure consistency in practice and information
- Contracts should include minimal performance expectations in a manner that is transparent and understood by all participating parties
- Failure mode analysis is an essential step in technology implementation prior to production use

Chapter 7

Trained as Planned

Nursing Documentation

Editor: E. Rose, MD

Key Words: Change management, clinicians, competency assessment, electronic health record (EHR) training,

Project Categories: inpatient electronic health record (EHR)

Lessons Learned Categories: communication, leadership, project management

Case Study

We have all heard about the importance of user participation in selection and implementation of clinical information systems. Several years ago this was a fundamental principle used by my team to identify units to test our electronic documentation system. Each unit selected was required to have an adequate staffing level, a low turnover rate, high morale, and full commitment to test our system for the specified test period. Interested units were told up front that each would be required to choose a core set of champions to train colleagues and lead the implementation of the change. Once units were selected, champions were identified by the nurse managers and trained by the study team. After full training, the champions assisted with training the remaining staff nurses and took responsibility for assessing and ensuring basic competency of each before go-live. A unit was not allowed to go live until all nurses were considered to be fully trained and competent.

During routine evaluations 3 months after go-live, we were surprised to learn that some of the nurses could not perform even the simplest functions that had been "required competencies" in the training. Also, many of the nurses reported not hearing about the change prior to attending the first mandatory training sessions even though we had open meetings describing our participation criteria. The training consisted of 4 hours in class and 4 hours of independent study, with each member required to pass a written test and return demonstration to demonstrate competency. After probing deeper, we discovered that competencies were not tracked or evaluated consistently by each unit's champions. One major discrepancy was that some champions allowed the staff nurses to report being competent rather than insist on the required demonstration. This fueled negative feelings about the documentation system being tested that in turn affected overall satisfaction of the users. In one instance, improper use of the system by one nurse adversely affected the quality of information available to the next nurse. In the end, costly retraining was needed to put the group back on track to offset this preventable outcome.

Author's Analysis

The most important lesson we learned was one we thought we already knew—training is critical to the success of a system. Doing training correctly, however, is not so simple for a variety of reasons. Hospitals are constantly undergoing change, and it is difficult to ensure that all staff have adequate knowledge and competency to carry it out because of the nature of how a hospital arranges for staffing (for example, full time, part time, resource pools, floaters, affiliate staff). Moreover, asking individuals (champions) to take responsibility for ensuring compliance of their peers' actions is problematic in the absence of an explicit mechanism for handling non-compliance. Because we wanted our units to own the change, we fostered "participation" by allowing each unit, under the direction of the manager, to tailor the training materials to fit the setting needs. Our mistake was to assume that the competency and commitment of the nurse manager and champions was sufficient to carry out the training properly.

On reflection, it is clear that the dynamic nature of the hospital environment coupled with continuous change contributes to the bending of rules to meet deadlines. This bending may be well meaning but can lead to unintended consequences. For example, in this scenario, we understood why champions trusted colleagues' "self reports" of competency, rather than requiring a demonstration of it because of time constraints. To address this issue, we have subsequently concentrated heavily on facilitating the creation of a training plan that is both feasible and effective and providing the necessary resources to develop and implement it. Funding excellent planning is as important as the training itself.

Editor's Commentary (E. Rose, MD)

This story about training is certainly sobering. Its teller, even at the time the story takes place, is no dilettante or neophyte in the world of complex HIT projects, but rather a seasoned professional, schooled in the formal and informal knowledge of the field. The plan was a page right out of enlightened project management, driving ownership of the project down as far to the end users as possible. This approach is supposed to get results and "empower" users at the same time. So can we learn anything from this story, or do we just throw up our hands and declare "The best-laid schemes of mice and men go oft astray"?

That overused quotation may itself hold the key to a lesson this story can teach us: In HIT implementations we must plan for failure. In HIT, no plan, however carefully or wisely it is crafted, allows a "set it and forget it" approach. Each project is unique and requires careful and close monitoring from its initiation, intensely at first, and less so as things appear more and more to go according to plan.

That being said, what differences in the plan, or its execution, might have produced a better outcome, or alerted the project leaders to the risk of an undesirable outcome?

One question is whether the "right" units were really selected. It is often difficult to determine what areas in an organization are ideal for testing new technology. The stated selection criteria for units to participate in the test project (adequate staffing, high morale, and so on) seem logical enough. However, one wonders whether the "full commitment to test" the system was shared by all throughout the unit. Managers may, at times, be motivated to adopt a new technology for a variety of reasons (curiosity, enthusiasm for the potential of the technology—in some cases, with exaggerated expectations as to the benefits it will bring, anticipated elevation of status as an innovator, and so on) despite a lack of readiness in their units or departments for the technology. Looking more closely at the units whose managers volunteered for this project might have called some of them into question as candidate units. Admittedly, however, in projects such as the one described here, the perception of the unit managers may be that they are extending a "favor" by their willingness to participate, and questioning their units' fitness might be politically sensitive.

Another question lies in the selection of "champions." Much has been written on the ideal characteristics of a "user champion" in complex technology deployments. There are few data from rigorous, controlled studies on this issue. However, general consensus exists that technology skills are a lesser predictor of success as a "champion" than respect and influence among the user community. The case history does not discuss how the champions were selected, but if the champions were self-selected through a volunteer process, or hand-selected by managers based on perceived information technology knowledge, they may have faced significant barriers to success. Given the dependence of the project on direct accountability of users to the champions for demonstrating competence with the system, the champions, when faced with resistance on the part of more senior and/or politically influential colleagues among the rank-and-file users, may have felt inhibited from attempting to force the issue of demonstrating competence.

Lessons Learned

- Continuously monitor projects for progress and desired outcomes
- Plan training programs and provide ongoing training options for effective outcomes
- Identify the "right" project champions

Chapter 8

Device Selection: No Other Phase Is More Important

Mobile Nursing Devices

Editor: G. Keenan, PhD, RN

Key Words: mobile devices, selection process, user opinions, workflow

Project Categories: infrastructure and technology

Lessons Learned Categories: leadership, project management, workflow

Case Study

Our story began almost 2 years ago. As a consultant, this author participated in a team that completed a device needs assessment for the selection of point of care documentation devices for Big Healthcare System (BHS). Our consultant team was engaged because of an unsatisfactory response from an employee to a member of the facility's board of directors. The question was "How did we arrive at the decision to select these certain machines that you are asking $1.7 million to purchase?"

Our team defined the following metrics for device selection:

- device form factor analysis (workstations on wheels, or WOWs), tablets, other handheld devices)
- space availability within patient rooms during use and storage
- provisions for spare machines
- downtime strategies
- analysis of various clinician usage and preferences

- wireless networking capacity and coverage
- integration with bar coding and scanning technologies
- electrical outlet availability (location and quantity)
- reallocation of existing desktop machines for physician usage

In total, this process was completed over the course of 8 weeks, and upon presentation to the board of directors, our team literally received a standing ovation. Upon completion of our work, we presented our strategy and success around device selection, and the abstract of this write-up received a national award.

Based on this success, there was great confidence in our processes. In a new opportunity for a similar device selection process as part of a larger project at a Regional Community Hospital (RCH) in the West, we expected to repeat our success. The project was initiated, and RCH built a team of invested, skilled, and knowledgeable clinical and information technology staff. However, the device selection team was scheduled to meet weekly, as opposed to the concentrated "all hands on deck" efforts experienced at BHS. Thus, from the project design stage, the process was changed to be longer in duration at RCH than our process of 8 weeks at BHS. Almost 2 years later, point-of-care devices were only just being purchased for use by nursing assistants, respiratory care thera-pists, and some sporadic use in the intensive care unit.

As a result of the slower, comprehensive, and methodical process for device selection, we identified opportunities that would not have been possible in a quicker, more concentrated project. Some of our notable findings are the following:

- the emergence of newer point-of-care technologies (tablets with scanners)
- postponement of capital expenditures
- reconciling specific challenges with wireless network coverage and capacity constraints
- resolution of infection control issues related to device cleaning and storage
- planning for medication administration and pharmacy delivery pro-cess changes
- configuration of WOWs

This methodical approach created a new challenge to our credibility, especially among the nursing staff. Because significant aspects of point-of-care device selection require participation from front-line nursing staff, we engaged the nursing staff early in the selection approval process. Although early involvement provided education and buy-in, it also led to significant delays in acquisition and deployment, which caused frustration among the nursing staff.

Author's Analysis

The single most important lesson learned is that the desired outcomes should dictate the duration and method of the decision-making process that is needed when selecting point-of-care devices. Both short and prolonged decision-making processes bring benefits and challenges. For example, the singular decisions and delays that occurred at RCH actually translated into a number of benefits. The selection team was able to develop a better understanding of the nurses' needs and to value their input; that resulted in greater buy-in among the nurses. On the other hand, the cumulative nature of the delays was a source of frustration, causing the team to appear inept and adversely influencing the senior management's perceptions of the validity of the team's recommendations. While this manuscript was being written, we neared what we hoped would be the end of the device selection and acquisition cycle. We designed a phased purchase and implementation planned to occur over the course of the next 6 months. This should allow for device storage, power management, and configuration as well as education, training, and workflow redesign for pharmacy and nursing staff.

Should this author participate in a similar project in the future, the experiences at both organizations will serve well. Point-of-care device selection timelines can and should be set by the interdisciplinary device selection team. While this team adhered to their mission, the practical objectives were missed because of a strict interpretation.

Editor's Commentary (G. Keenan, PhD, RN)

This case study provides a great example of why it is important to fit the decision-making process to the purpose and desired outcomes of the decision and not be single minded about the length of the timeline. Because conventional wisdom extols the merits of "decisiveness," it is no surprise that most would favor the short process of BHS in device selection if given the choice between it and the longer RCH process.

Certainly the extra costs of a longer process alone provide "immediate" and powerful evidence that when presented will quickly squelch any interest in engaging in a more involved and longer selection process.

Most would agree, however, that our health technology decisions have a dramatic impact on the delivery of care and once made cannot be easily reversed. It thus is absolutely essential that the very best decisions be made in the selection phase because this is the only phase in which the purchase of a bad system can be prevented and the associated costs abated. The piece most frequently given the least attention in the selection phase is the expected impact of technology on the user, whose work should be made easier, safer, more efficient, and effective. In this scenario RCH was more cognizant of the people issues than BCH. Nonetheless, the case study did indicate that RCH lacked a rational strategy for how to incorporate the "people side" into the selection. RCH focused on learning the nurses' opinions about and getting buy-in for a system that the user had not tested under real-time conditions. Clinicians' opinions of systems that have not been fully tested under real-time conditions should not be treated as conclusive evidence of the benefits and value of the system. To remedy this repeating problem, I recommend that all organizations engage in a process by which the products being reviewed are tested under simulated conditions in a clinical setting. In this way, organizations will discover the overt and covert impact of these devices on the users and the system at large.

Lessons Learned

- Structure a decision-making process to achieve the desired outcomes and communicate this to participants
- The "selection" phase is the critical phase to prevent the purchase of bad technology; invest time and money to be very thoughtful about HIT selection
- The opinions of users about products they have never used under real-time conditions are not solid evidence of the value of an information technology device;
  - Simulate the impact of devices during evaluation under real-time conditions to better understand the effect on users and the care delivery system as a whole

Chapter 9

If It Ain't Broke, Don't Fix It

Replacing an HIS

Editor: L. Ozeran, MD

Key Words: best of breed, challenge assumptions, portal, open architecture, single vendor solution, strategy, workflow

Project Categories: inpatient electronic health record (EHR)

Lessons Learned Categories: leadership, system design, workflow

Case Study

Prompted by the inaugural staffing of its new chief information officer (CIO) position (after a 2-year search!), our large academic medical center reassessed the best-of-breed clinical information systems strategy it had pursued previously. We had implemented an open-architecture clinical data repository with an efficient portal for clinicians to review repository data, maintaining access to data in other systems. Under the new direction, we would actively pursue a single-vendor strategy as much as possible.

A request for proposal (RFP) was issued, and respondents were culled to a "short list" of major vendors offering large product suites. Each vendor gave an in-house demonstration, and each vendor's premier client site was visited. Participants in the demonstrations and visits (principally clinicians of all stripes and a range of administrators) provided feedback to an RFP evaluation committee, the majority of whom were administrators. The clinicians' strong consensus was that Vendor X's system (using a relatively closed architecture) had the least functional and least efficient clinician portal, nursing documentation system, and clinical data repository, whereas Vendor Y – supplier of the institution's existing systems in these areas – had the strongest products. However, because of the range of other products in the solution set it offered, as well as other administrative considerations (for example, larger company size), Vendor X was selected by the committee.

First, the institution's obsolete best-of-breed pharmacy system was replaced with Vendor X's pharmacy system. Next, development was undertaken simultaneously on Vendor X's nursing system, clinician portal, and clinical data repository (replacing Vendor Y's equivalent systems). Because it initially appeared that information entered into Vendor X's nursing system could be viewed only in Vendor X's portal, plans were made to deploy both systems in tandem on a ward-by-ward basis over a period of several weeks.

Concerns developed during the local development and configuration of Vendor X's nursing and portal systems, which seemed unimproved since the RFP demonstrations 3 years earlier. Casual testing of the impact of switching from Vendor Y's portal to Vendor X's portal demonstrated a significant loss of clinician efficiency. The time required to retrieve and understand a given body of results varied from approximately twofold to tenfold depending on the extent of the result set. Clinicians were concerned that without the luxury of seeing fewer patients, their existing limited time for data review might potentially result in diagnostic and therapeutic delays and errors.

Nevertheless, to promote the institutional benefits of a single-vendor strategy, we activated the new repository and began to implement the nursing and portal systems. Nurses indicated that their new system was weaker than Vendor Y's system but was tolerable. Physician portal users (including residents, physician extenders, and medical students) expressed substantial dislike for their new portal, but it was hoped that this assessment was merely an adjustment reaction. Implementation proceeded throughout the wards, with clinicians making workflow adjustments as necessary (for example, rounding without information on current vital signs because data collection was either too time-consuming or in fact impossible). However, on the first attempt to go live in one of the intensive care units, the new portal's deficiencies led to a serious reduction in patient care quality. The intensivists' understanding of their patients' conditions deteriorated so precipitously that go-live was halted after 4 days, workflow was reverted to prior procedures, and further analysis was undertaken to determine if the product's deficiencies could be satisfactorily addressed.

Analysis showed that the new portal's deficiencies could not be rectified using the current version of the product. Discussions with the vendor indicated that sufficient improvements would not be available for at least a few years.

The new portal was deemed an institutional failure.

Alternative approaches were quickly identified and evaluated. One option was to adopt the latest version of Vendor Y's product, a substantial enhancement over our older version; we had deferred numerous upgrades because of uncertainty about our strategy. After 15 years successfully interfacing numerous ancillary systems to Vendor Y's open architecture portal, we found that Vendor X's ancillary systems (for example, nursing and medication administration) could be interfaced to Vendor Y's portal. The clinical community again concluded Vendor Y's portal was the preferred product. Leadership nimbly switched gears and struck a deal with Vendor Y to rapidly implement not only its upgraded portal but also some newer modules, including an open architecture clinical data mining package that will serve not only our institution but also a developing statewide consortium of academic medical centers. Our decision to retain an open architecture repository was soon serendipitously reinforced by the emergence of an independently developed plan for a health information exchange in which clinical systems from our institution and several regional competitors will be linked to improve patient care.

Author's Analysis

Many lessons have been learned or reinforced during this odyssey. Our "top five" are as follows:

First, "don't fix what ain't broke." Vendor Y's systems had long worked well. Their architecture was well suited to an academic environment in need of best-of-breed ancillary systems and was highly efficient for review of the voluminous data pool created by testing performed on complex tertiary patients. Vendor X's portal was determined early on to be significantly inferior to Vendor Y's portal for our needs. In retrospect, a more careful consideration of the possibility of continuing to use Vendor Y's portal may have helped.

Second, busy clinicians highly value their time and thus prize tools that improve their efficiency. Clinicians' needs are served well by carefully assessing in advance the efficiency of new tools proposed for their use. Tools for clinicians that do not improve efficiency should be examined critically prior to adoption; tools that significantly worsen efficiency require remarkable benefits elsewhere in the organization, to justify adoption.

Third, user opinion ("the will of the people") is discounted at one's peril. Clinicians who previewed Vendor X's suite during the RFP demonstrations were unanimously opposed to their portal, an opinion discounted by the administrator-heavy RFP evaluation committee. In retrospect, it was not surprising (and thus avoidable) that Vendor X's portal was poorly received during initial implementation and ultimately deemed a failure.

Fourth, understanding expectations prior to deployment of a new system can help avoid disappointments and failures. Vendor X was perplexed by our dislike for its portal. They claimed that all of their other customers had received it well, but admitted those customers had never had a portal before, possibly facilitating their perception of Vendor X's portal as an improvement. Also, Vendor X never analyzed Vendor Y's portal and our clinicians' use of it, thus failing to discover in advance that the replacement would be a net downgrade. As soon as it became apparent that improvement was not forthcoming, disappointment and failure became highly likely.

Fifth, flexibility is crucial. As portal implementation was ultimately unsuccessful, we discovered centers similar to ours that had learned to use Vendor X's nonportal products with their own portals. Rather than persist with an ineffective portal, our leadership quickly leveraged this discovery and switched to a more successful path.

We hope other healthcare institutions—and HIT vendors—will learn from our experience and avoid similar errors in the future.

Editor's Commentary (L. Ozeran, MD)

Where to begin? So many things went wrong and yet the overlying answer should be to challenge your assumptions. The CIO assumed that a single vendor solution would be better than a multivendor approach. When things weren't going well, that would have been a good time to reassess. Hospital administration assumed that clinicians would overcome their dislike of the system and be compliant with whatever the institution bought. There was an assumption that the portal would improve in the 3 years from demonstration of the product to its implementation.

Clinicians assumed they could not spend more time reviewing the data or get a workaround (for example, chart printout) from hospital staff. In addition to other assumptions, the information technology department assumed that the new vendor's modules could be implemented in phases, but the advantage of a single vendor became problematic, and some modules were dependent on the existence of others.

The authors should be applauded for sharing this story because there is anecdotal evidence suggesting that this scenario occurs frequently but few are willing to talk about it. The most difficult aspect of challenging your assumptions is realizing that you are making an assumption. This is where it can be helpful to identify knowledgeable, reliable, honest people within your organization to ask periodically if what you are doing still makes sense. Make those queries part of your process by making them an appointment on your project timeline and plan. Ongoing bidirectional communication is a critical element of success. Keep open the lines of communication with all stakeholders. When there is significant disagreement among stakeholders, as happened in this case study, consider bringing in an experienced consultant to provide an independent point of view. However, when the stakeholders who are expected to use the system are overruled by those who manage the system, beware.

Lessons Learned

- "Don't fix what ain't broke."
- Remember that clinicians prize tools that improve efficiency.
- Do not discount clinician input
- Understand expectations prior to technology deployment
- Always keep open lines of communication
- Be flexible

Chapter 10

Effective Leadership Includes the Right People

Informatics Expertise

Editor: G. Keenan, PhD, RN

Key Words: change, electronic health record (EHR), informatics specialist, information technology (IT) decisions, organizational culture,

Project Categories: inpatient electronic health record (EHR)

Lessons Learned Categories: data model, leadership, system configuration

Case Study

A long-standing medical college and hospital with a proud history of innovation, which nearly went bankrupt, was acquired and saved by a university and a national for-profit hospital chain company. The university acquiring the medical college lacked healthcare experience. The acquired hospital had been nonprofit in its century of existence, and the takeover by a for-profit chain was somewhat of a shock to its faculty and staff. The ultimate solution, however, was better than other alternatives discussed before the takeover—including turning the facility into condominiums.

Merging the cultures of the medical college and university was proving a challenge. A culture of mistrust and anxiety about cross-college collaborations with the acquiring university seemed to prevail at the medical college. It certainly did not help when a managerial and financial "firewall" was set up between the university and the healthcare campus, so that any financial trouble in the healthcare units would not cross over to the university. The acquired managed-care-owned hospital, once part of a proud and unified academic medical center, was now largely "off limits" to management of either the medical college or university. Moreover, the acquiring for-profit hospital chain owner was losing money and divesting itself of some of the chain's local hospitals.

A medical informatics specialist with significant experience in design and implementation of clinical IT in nearby large medical centers was hired by the main university, but with a primary appointment in a computer and information-related college and not the medical college. The informaticist was to develop an educational program in medical informatics to help set up cross-college collaborations in informatics research, and assist in other areas as needed.

The College of Medicine did not leverage the informaticist in the implementation of an electronic health record (EHR) for its for-profit faculty practice plan. The informaticist offered her services and the medical college's and faculty practice plan's dean, chief information officer (CIO), chief operations officer (COO), and other top executives were well aware of her background. Because of existing sociocultural issues that divided the acquired medical campus and the acquiring university (mostly in the domain of distrust—and perhaps disdain), the informaticist's services or advice were not utilized.

Here is a summarized report from an HIT blog:

A posted record of lawsuit was filed against the EHR vendor by the University's College of Medicine's for-profit practice group, claiming that the EHR 'does not function per the specifications provided.' The lawsuit accused the vendor of breach of contract, fraud, and other contractual shortcomings. Over $1 million was paid for the system, and problems with claims billing cost the practice group twice that amount. The university filed an injunction requiring the EHR vendor to provide a system that performs evaluation and management (E/M or billing) coding or pay professional coders to do the job. One example they cited: no Review of Systems template existed for the E/M coder that handles allergy/immunologic or hematologic/lymphatic organ systems. They provided confirmation from the EHR vendor that certain aspects of the EHR did not function properly.

The informaticist had direct and relevant experience in EHR implementation and would have recommended extensive testing of the financial components before go-live. She had observed similar happenings at a different university, where a different faculty practice plan and vendor's defective products collided and resulted in a U.S. Department of Justice investigation, a large fine, admission by the university that it lacked the appropriate IT management depth, and complete abandonment of a multimillion-dollar IT investment because of resultant defective billing practices.

Author's Analysis

The lessons are that informatics specialists should be aware of the challenges of integrating cultures of healthcare systems and non-healthcare components of universities. Informatics experts should be aware that their expertise may be regarded as unneeded or perhaps frightening to officials in charge of EHR implementation, who often lack medical backgrounds and are being asked to do much more than they are really capable of doing. Informaticists should educate hospital and university officials that not knowing what you don't know about complex EHR issues, and placing too much trust in vendor promises, can lead to system failure – or worse.

Editor's Commentary (G. Keenan, PhD, RN)

The merging of very different cultures under a single umbrella is problematic, especially during the period immediately following a takeover. Moreover, if no plan or actions are taken to unify the diverse entities into a productive whole, the entities are likely to remain at odds indefinitely. This translates into employees working at cross purposes or not being utilized when appropriate, resulting in increasing associated costs. This seems to have been the situation described in the case study. It is unfortunate that the medical informatics specialist, given her background, was not tapped for her expertise in EHRs even though she offered assistance. In organizations with effective cultures, individuals recognize their strengths and weaknesses and do what it takes to find and utilize the best expertise to solve group problems. This did not happen in the organization described in the case study.

There are a number of possible perspectives that one might consider to achieve a better outcome in a similar situation; two will be discussed here. The first is to avoid working for organizations that have ineffective cultures. These actually can be spotted during the interview phase. It is recommended that one talk with as many potential colleagues in an organization to assess a match with the values and ways business is conducted and problems are solved. Colleagues at higher and lower levels as well as in departments with which one might expect to collaborate should be interviewed. If the fit seems poor, you are likely to be continually frustrated unless you hold a top position of influence within your area of expertise (or have the support of the person who does).

A second perspective would be to take the job but with a solid proactive approach about how you will work effectively within the organization to improve the culture. For example, as a condition for employment, you could stipulate in your contract that you would be given the option to serve as a member on all committees that focus on the EHR within the health-related colleges and affiliated hospitals. Also, you could begin to nurture relationships with colleagues of like mind who eventually could work together to move IT actions and policy in the desired direction.

There is one other consideration. Sometimes those responsible for making HIT decisions but unqualified to make those decisions are insecure in their positions, leading to their distrust of local experts. These leaders have no way of knowing whether the local expert is acting in the best interest of the institution or their own best interest. This is a common local expert phenomenon not limited to HIT. When this occurs, it can sometimes be mitigated by bringing in an outside consultant (from more than 50 miles away is suggested by "common" wisdom). When the disinterested outside expert provides advice similar to the local expert, it may help improve local trust and recognition.

Lessons Learned

- The individuals with the most expertise in IT are not always the ones making the important IT decisions.
- Organizations must have clearly defined strategic goals and tactical objectives that are conducive to the success of broad HIT initiatives
- Informaticists should carefully evaluate the culture of an organization when considering employment
- Poorly led or poorly designed HIT initiatives can have broad and deep negative impacts across a health system

Part II
Ambulatory Care Focus

Chapter 11

Leadership and Strategy

An Ambulatory EHR

Editor: L. Ozeran, MD

Key Words: electronic health record (EHR), enterprise strategy, physician champion, project management, vision

Project Categories: ambulatory electronic health record (EHR)

Lessons Learned Categories: leadership, project management, staffing resources

Case Study

Whether it is your first bicycle ride, your first date, or the first step your child takes, you never forget your *'first time'*. I will never forget my first installation of an electronic health record (EHR): it was an utter failure.

In the early 1990s, as a full-time faculty physician in infectious disease, my employer was a multihospital system in a major metropolitan area. Among many other facilities, the system operated methadone maintenance and treatment programs. We were awarded a grant to provide primary human immunodeficiency virus (HIV) care to former substance users in the inner city, a public-private initiative to improve healthcare to one especially underserved focus of the HIV epidemic.

As medical director for the grant programs, collecting and reporting grant-required specifications was my job. We provided a standard of care reflecting the best evidence-based medicine at the time: HIV monitoring (CD4 counts), antiretroviral therapy, prophylaxis to prevent

59

opportunistic infection, screening and treatment for tuberculosis, screening for chlamydia and gonorrhea, periodic Pap smears, and mental health assessment were among the key standards tracked for the grant.

We deployed the most commonly used technology for clinical data capture at the time: paper forms. Despite our best efforts, data discrepancies began to appear. Patients sometimes arrived for urgent visits when their charts were elsewhere. Medication refills by phone created progress notes and addenda that were not always collated with the chart in a timely fashion.

Our wonderful paper forms did not always reflect the degree of care provided. No matter how many check boxes we had, how complete the requested data set, or how bright the color of paper, many staff would not update the paper form completely each and every time. It came to pass that I would scour each chart every month to monitor compliance. It was not only time-consuming but I sensed that even with my best efforts a key datum might escape my notice in the growing number of paper charts and forms.

It seemed that an EHR could capture medications, CD4 counts, and conditions during the course of care, obviating the need for duplicate data entry on a data collection form. The EHR could manage a list of medications and print out prescriptions as needed. An ongoing problem list could be maintained. Simple queries could generate performance reports. Missing paper charts would be but distant memories of the past.

We had no formal software process. With the quality committee's approval, we sought software and hardware for an EHR with our grant re-funding application. Once funding was approved, we simply selected one of the better known products. As time drew near to purchase the EHR, I was confident the project would be a complete success. Our clinical team wanted the EHR. The grant sponsor approved our budget modification. What could go wrong?

For starters, the project champion would leave.

Unexpectedly, I was offered and took another job opportunity within the system. I would no longer work on the EHR project but I had a colleague who was more of a technophile than I. Confidently passing the baton to my friend, I was unaware that being a successful change agent requires skills different from a facility with technology.

With a Joint Commission hospital survey coming, I was thrown into my new position with little time to follow the new EHR project. After the Joint Commission survey, I took the opportunity to check up on my old friends in the HIV primary care program. I was surprised to learn that neither the software nor hardware was installed. The same paper-based charts that preceded my departure remained in place. Nothing had changed. What went wrong?

Author's Analysis

As someone recently stated before the Certifying Commission for Health Information Technology, "Adoption of an EHR is an ugly, ugly process. (Pizzi 2007)," but it is not just EHR adoption. According to a 2002 report from the National Institute of Standards and Technology, up to 25 percent of commercial software projects are abandoned before completion. Project failure is not uncommon in IT inside or outside of healthcare (RTI Health, Social, and Economics Research 2002).

The literature is replete with advice on how to avoid failure. John Glaser describes critical success factors for clinical information systems that apply to our failed EHR project (Glaser 2005).

1. Strong organizational vision and strategy.

2. Talented and committed leadership.

3. A partnership between the clinical, administrative, and information technology (IT) staffs.

4. Excellent implementation skills, especially in project management and support.

Although my section chief and department chair gave formal approval to the EHR project and my colleague replacing me as project champion agreed with my personal vision, there was no enterprise EHR strategy.

The project was conceived and submitted without the knowledge, advice, or consent of our IT staff. They learned of the project only after its approval.

No one on our EHR team had IT project management experience. Without project management expertise, any IT project is at risk.

After 10 years of informatics experience, I now know that the odds were against this particular ambulatory EHR project. Neither the time nor environment was right for it yet. Too many of the critical success factors were missing for it to have turned out any other way.

Editor's Commentary (L. Ozeran, MD)

It is regrettably common for well-meaning, smart people to underestimate what is required to accomplish a successful IT implementation, both in and out of healthcare. In this case, some critical aspects were present: a physician champion, supportive leadership, and adequate funding. The key project faults were not clearly articulating the project's needs through a needs assessment and gap analysis before selecting products, and not involving all of the stakeholders, most notably IT staff. As a relatively isolated, focused project, having an enterprise EHR strategy may have made the project more cost effective, but probably was not necessary for the project to succeed.

Without additional details about the specifics of the environment, it is just as hard now to determine what should have been done as it was then. We do not know the number of physical locations, which staff would access the system, what authentication would be needed, and how functional privileges would be allocated. In the absence of specifics, we can only return to generic recommendations to add to those described by Glaser:

5. Identify all stakeholders, educate them about technology specific to the project, and seek their input; this does not appear to have been done for this project.

6. Clearly state what the system is to accomplish in several detailed statements; in this project, there seemed only a general outline of what was to be accomplished.

7. Compare what technology you currently have to what you need to accomplish those stated goals (your gap analysis); apparently this was not done.

8. Determine your budget (this was done) and how much of your goals you can accomplish with that money.

9. Create lists of features and functions that support your goals and use them to determine which products can best meet your needs within your budget; this does not appear to have been done.

10. Define scripts that you can follow to test the validity of vendor claims in your environment and run them against the three most likely candidates; there does not appear to have been any due diligence

done for the vendor selling the product selected or a comparison of the project needs to the product selected or to any other products for that matter.

Had these issues been addressed in addition to the positive factors that were accomplished (for example, having an effective physician champion, adequate funding, supportive leadership), the project would have been much more likely to have succeeded.

Lessons Learned

- Articulate a clear project (and enterprise) strategy and project plan including timeline and desired outcomes
- Perform a needs assessment prior to product selection
- Involve all stakeholders in the decision-making process, including clinicians, administrators, IT staff, and anyone else who may 'touch' the planned system; administrative support is critical.
- Evaluate several products or solutions with tests comparable to use in your actual environment

Chapter 12

Designing Custom Software for Quality Reports

An EHR for a Community Health Center

Editor: B. Gugerty, DNS, MS, RN

Key Words: ambulatory electronic health record (EHR), database structure, data mining, disease management, primary care, quality improvement, scope

Project Categories: ambulatory electronic health record (EHR)

Lessons Learned Categories: data model, project management

Case Study

Our federally-qualified health center (FQHC) wanted an EHR that would allow aggregate analysis of care and streamline encounter billing. In 1996, there were very few good, affordable EHRs appropriate for a small practice, so "the deciders" hired a young, ambitious software programmer and we four primary care nurse practitioners consulted in the design of a clinical and billing program that was to be for in-house use only. The programmer assured everyone that he could do the work in about 6 months! Over the next 4 years, in addition to maintaining the volume of patient care, we analyzed workflow, selected data to be captured, classified data elements as to coding systems and relationships, and iteratively tested the developing EHR. The program was written in structured query language (SQL) with open database connectivity (ODBC). We emphasized to the programmer that, in order to use the data for quality improvement, we needed structured data entry, standardized terminology, a user interface to promote consistent data entry, and a relational database that would link diagnoses, interventions, and outcomes. We were especially interested in capturing primary care interventions of patient education and case management, in addition to medications, procedures, and follow up.

When the clinical software was ready and we went "live" to document encounters, we still could not print prescriptions, download electronic laboratory results, or trigger encounter bills. Nevertheless, the expanded programming team arranged for necessary hardware and networks, directed staff training, scheduled implementation and archival data entry, and provided technical support—when they weren't selling the software to other health centers. We went "live" all at once, in December 1999. Data were stored on a server in the main site that was accessible remotely by dial-up modem with password protection. After documenting a full 6 months of primary care, I received funding to study the reliability of the data for quality assessment. Quality audits that I did with a Crystal Reports expert were extremely challenging because of the lack of a data dictionary and the data table structure that had grown "like topsy." Furthermore, the in-house programmers, who were busy marketing the software, were not available to trouble-shoot. The report expert had to determine by himself which of several database maps he was given actually matched the existing database structure.

The quality audits that we managed to generate revealed that diagnoses, interventions, and outcomes were not linked, much terminology was inconsistent and nonstandard, and differing data entry patterns had resulted in scrambled data storage. Therefore, we could not verify that patients with chronic illness received care according to national guidelines, or that preventive care such as cancer screening was properly and promptly followed up. For example, interventions recorded for 30 patients with diabetes showed patient education that included the following information: 5 stop smoking, 3 nutrition, 4 diet, 5 exercise, 2 weight loss, 5 chronic illness, 7 diabetic care, 7 sign/symptom of illness, 12 other. Definitions for these suspiciously overlapping interventions were nonexistent. Without a laboratory interface and discrete variables for cholesterol, glycosylated hemoglobin, or urine microalbumin results, and with inconsistent data entry and database storage, aggregate data could not be retrieved. Similar issues were found for hypertensive and depressed patients seen over the period. In addition, data mining for appropriate follow-up of Pap smears was not reliable for quality assessment, because of inconsistent documentation of laboratory results and text notes of the follow-up plan.

Author's Analysis

Our lessons learned are right in line with Bakken's "five building blocks of an informatics infrastructure for evidence-based practice...":

1. Standardized terminologies and structures

2. Digital sources of evidence

3. Standards that facilitate healthcare data exchange among heterogeneous systems

4. Informatics processes that support the acquisition and application of evidence to a specific clinical situation

5. Informatics competencies (Bakken 2001)

Digital sources of evidence include EHRs equipped with appropriate standardized terminologies and operated by healthcare providers who are competent in data entry. Data mining from EHRs is extremely difficult without defined, standardized terminologies. In this case, the provider /users were limited by insufficient knowledge of structured language and database design. The programmer had no prior experience in healthcare. Lack of agency resources reduced iterative software development and the potential for group learning. Furthermore, programming to create key labor-saving capabilities for e-prescribing, electronic download of laboratory results, guideline-based templates to remind and record orders for common encounters, automatic tracking for follow-up visits, a flow sheet of interventions given, and interface to billing was never accomplished. Nevertheless, appropriate interventions documented over 6 months for diabetes, hypertension, and depression did include health teaching, guidance, and counseling; case management and referral; procedures; and medications.

The resulting EHR was essentially a resource-intensive exercise in creating and implementing a rough beta version of software that worked fairly well for individual patient documentation but that was totally unacceptable for quality assessment and improvement. Much of the potential of electronic data aggregation for practice evaluation was lost in a provider focus on individual care. Although the primary care providers had each learned the research process and frequently read clinical research articles, the EHR was not seen as a tool for research and evaluation. Fundamental rules of research, such as identification and definition of key data elements, accurate data entry, and advance planning for analyses, were lost in the challenge of software development during day-to-day clinical care responsibilities. Clinical consciousness did not expand to research consciousness as the EHR developed.

Using informatics to build evidence from clinical practice has great potential to enhance our understanding of the most valuable and effective interventions in primary healthcare, in the face of expanding demand and shrinking supply of providers and payment. Furthermore, integrating decision support into documentation promises to promote "best practices" that are already known. The experience described here contributed a great deal to my own continuing education and my current involvement in efforts such as the Certification Committee for Healthcare Information Technology (CCHIT) and clinical informatics to improve public health.

Editor's Commentary (B. Gugherty, DNS, MS, RN)

The author states that "fundamental rules of research, such as identification and definition of key data elements, accurate data entry, and advance planning for analyses, were lost in the challenge of software development during day-to-day clinical care responsibilities." Thus, the original goals of the system "…aggregate analysis of care and streamline encounter billing…" were consequently and similarly "lost." The take-away message from this case study is that if you want to make sense of data and information in an EHR on the back end, it matters a great deal how you structure and input data on the front end. The author "got" that key lesson.

For a book about lessons learned from HIT failures, the case study presented here certainly illustrates failure well. Yet we are well advised to judge historical events and figures in the context of their times, not ours. The year 1996, when this effort was begun, is a bygone historical era if measured by Internet time. Yes, the Internet was invented well before 1996, but it was not until 1997 that it began to be truly widely adopted and used. Therefore, a first reaction to judge hiring ONE programmer to design and build a wide- ranging and multiple-module clinical and billing information system in 6 months as hopelessly naïve must be resisted. Especially in ambulatory care settings, these things were still being done in, as my son calls it, "the olden days."

There is evidence of much good thinking at the beginning of this effort and throughout to attempt to incorporate fundamental principles of data structuring and clinical terminologies, but again we have come a long way in this regard since 1999 when the system went live. So I cannot fault this team except that explicitly selecting a small set of clinical terminologies and making the effort to stick to that set when and where possible might have been helpful and should have been within their scope of expertise. SNOMED, CCC (known as HHCC in the 1990s) or NIC/NOC/NANDA, and of course the old standards ICD-9 and CPT were good candidates for this project.

The software developer on this project installed alpha, or at best beta code, and effectively abandoned it to go off to sell the software elsewhere. Vendors currently cannot get away with so flagrant a violation of good business practices, yet this "old" vivid story in microcosm some-times remains a problem with established information techonology (IT) vendors within, and beyond, healthcare. Sales are extremely important to the HIT vendor companies, as they should be, but sometimes in acqui-sition/sales processes that go awry, there can be significant mismatches with what the capabilities of the software are and the expectations of the customer of that software. The author's response, getting involved in the CCHIT EHR standards rather than being turned off from infor-matics completely, is commendable. The expertise from this early HIT initiative will be helpful to the author and many others. I would, how-ever, caution that CCHIT accreditation may be necessary but should not be sufficient to vigorously probe the vendors and the systems that they offer during an acquisition process; acquisition processes should scruti-nize the capabilities of existing HIT solutions and the expectation gap on several levels. In defense of the developer, there appears to have been significant scope creep during this project; expanding scope in both scale and complexity is common in HIT initiatives, especially as customers develop more sophisticated understanding of their own needs. Collabo-ration and transparent, honest communication between a vendor and customer are usually the best solutions to potential conflicts because of scope creep. A solid project plan and an experienced project manager, perhaps in the form of a third-party consultant, might have made a big difference by offering an objective viewpoint.

Lessons Learned

- Standardized terminologies and data sets are required for aggregate reporting.
- Digital sources of information facilitate standardized data capture.
- HIT will only deliver the functionality for which it is designed (that is, individual patient record compared with population-based reporting).
- It is rare that the complexity of an HIT initiative can be met by a single programmer.

Chapter 13

If It's Designed and Built by One, It Will Not Serve the Needs of Many

Custom-Developed EHR

Editor: S. Silverstein, MD

Key Words: communication, design, development, electronic health record (EHR), stakeholder participation,

Project Categories: inpatient electronic health record (EHR)

Lessons Learned Categories: leadership, staffing resources, workflow

Case Study

In the late 1980s, a young resident physician at a large hospital took a year from clinical duties for research activities. One of the specialty services wanted to collect patient information on a notebook computer. With a programming background and a long-standing interest in electronic medical records, the resident thought this would be a great opportunity.

There were brief discussions about who served as supervising attending and what the service wanted the program to do in general, but mostly the resident was left alone to pursue the dream. After the first month, the local system was able to connect to separate radiology, dictation, and laboratory systems. The local computer would login as a user, use recursive screen scraping routines (developed by the resident) to collect and filter the data and assign it to the correct patient. The attending was informed and seemed pleased.

During the remaining months, some time had to be spent doing other research activities, but their impact was limited on the EHR project. Being a DOS-based system, windowing options were limited, but a full screen approach was able to accept mouse clicks for cursor positioning and selection of menu items. A series of menus allowed the user to move from one patient to another, enter new patients, and pass between sections of a patient's chart.

The resident even developed a novel hierarchical encoding system for examination findings, patient complaints, anatomic regions, and so on. Two separate tools were created. One enabled authorized users to create ontologies in a hierarchical fashion that were represented in the 32-bit identifier itself, allowing data size to shrink and speed recovery of matching patients with direct and indirect matches for performing drug studies or other research. The other tool allowed viewing or selecting from the lists the users had created. There was no limit to the number of ontologies that could be created.

Multiple portions of the EHR came live: vital signs, a patient's daily fluid inputs/outputs with predefined fluids to pick from expandable lists, transferred data from other information systems, pick lists for patients, entry of new patients, and so on. The system was documented and one hospital employee was trained. The department purchased a notebook computer and, as far as the resident could tell, everything was working and ready to go. But was it?

When the resident physician graduated the residency program, the system had been used rarely, if at all.

Author's Analysis

The system was designed with the resident's skill set and needs in mind, not those of the ultimate user(s). The system was very advanced for its time, but perhaps too complicated for the user at the time. There seemed to be inadequate input from the other users about what they truly needed and how the system would work best for them.

In the end, a great opportunity for promoting HIT was lost because of inadequate communication with the stakeholders. Even when project technologists have clinical backgrounds, they do not speak for everyone.

Editor's Commentary (S. Silverstein, MD)

This case study of a single person's efforts to create innovative HIT is a microcosm that is representative of common problems that occur in healthcare information technology (IT) design and implementation by larger groups and by vendors.

The major issue is false assumptions about the needs, enthusiasm, desire to contribute time and effort, and ultimate drivers and motivators (or demotivators, such as fear of what robust data might reveal) of HIT end-users and other stakeholders. The example is especially relevant to the creation of customized IT for focused specialty areas or for biomedical research, but also applies to unremarkable HIT such as EHR and computerized provider order entry (CPOE) facilitating clinical care delivery.

A specialty service wanted to aggregate data drawn from larger systems for varied research purposes. The needs assessment and design discussions were brief and identified just one physician who was to act as a spokesperson for a larger group. Inadequate involvement of stakeholders through inadequate interaction, and/or selection of a "representative" or representatives whose own knowledge of true needs might be inadequate, or who might emphasize their own interests over others, is an error. It is a mistake that falls under the general category of underrepresentation of stakeholders. These stakeholders include users and those who are affected, or potentially affected, by the output or outcomes from information system deployment.

Introduction of new technologies often creates winners and losers in a competitive environment. Those who are left out, especially those who might perceive the technology as a threat and who are not given the opportunity to express this perception and negotiate, can become obstacles to project success (through passive or even active aggressive behaviors, for example).

This resident only explored others' needs briefly, and then was "left alone" to do things as he or she saw fit. Although IT personnel and vendors might find that situation desirable in order to complete a project within a limited time period, in the end it increases the risk of rejection and failure of the HIT project significantly. One person, even a healthcare domain expert (or worse, a nondomain expert such as a junior medical professional or a nonmedical IT professional) is an inadequate representative of the need for planning, design, acquisition, implementation, and life cycle enhancement of an HIT application. These are complex processes requiring adequate involvement of, and frequent collaboration between, IT personnel, clinical personnel, and often their management who control resources.

The medical resident (trainee) spent significant time developing an application and coding system innovative for its time. The system may have been far more advanced than other applications in use, with integrated ontology development and maintenance tools and no artificial limits on data complexity. The resident probably expected users to recognize its advanced nature and adopt it enthusiastically on the basis of its technological sophistication and elegance.

The reality was different. Few used the system, and only rarely. This was not paradoxical. Issues that could have contributed to the lack of acceptance and use, which currently remain unchanged, include:

- The system as designed might not actually meet the research needs of a variety of stakeholders, as design parameters were set by too few users (in this case, one).

- The designer's own assumptions may not have been correct for the situation.

- The designer may have overestimated the ability, desire, and resources available for users to learn the system and integrate it into their daily workflows.

- The system might have been excellent technically, but difficult and cryptic to those for whom it was made. Iterative and incremental development processes with involvement of a variety of end users might yield a more satisfactory user experience.

- Only one person was trained in use of the system. There was a lack of training of others as backups or independent users. Inadequate training, in numbers and depth, is a common cause of end user difficulty and rejection of HIT. It may have been assumed that the one employee who was trained would then pass this knowledge to others. This is not a good assumption in the complex and competitive world of biomedicine.

A major lesson that can be learned from this case is the need for adequate user and stakeholder participation in all phases of HIT design, development, and deployment. This differs from the more traditional management information systems development process, which is often done in relative isolation after an initial assessment and design phase.

Another lesson that should be learned is the need for HIT project leaders and key personnel to not allow their own biases and assumptions to color the deliverables. This will too often occur in a manner that makes sense to them from their other expertise and experience, but might create a very unsatisfactory and unproductive user experience, and a distraction from other important work, for those "in the trenches" who have to do the actual healthcare work.

Lessons Learned

- Design for the needs of end-users (clinicians) as a group
- Involve clinicians in system design
- Plan to integrate systems into clinicians' workflows
- Train end-users in sufficient quantity and depth of knowledge of a technology to enable peer learning and peer support for use of HIT

Chapter 14

Clinician Adoption

Community-Based EHR

Editor: L. Ozeran, MD

Key Words: communication, end-user training, organizational change, human-computer interaction, implementation, primary care, workflow

Project Categories: ambulatory electronic health record (EHR), computerized provider order entry (CPOE), inpatient electronic health record (EHR)

Lessons Learned Categories: communication, leadership, technology problems, training, workflow

Case Study

Integration of computer-based patient records has recently been initiated in our country involving the entire infrastructure for patient-related data management and interconnecting previously isolated systems. In order to address this issue, a county council is in the process of implementing an EHR that will allow primary healthcare centers (PHCs), hospitals, and pharmacies to be integrated and able to exchange patient information. The system provides an infrastructure for sharing patient data and information between all care providers in the healthcare area. The system consists of three parts: drug information, which consists of information about all of the patients' medications and prescription-support functions, and is used to send electronic prescriptions; care documentation, which consists of all patient notes from physicians, nurses, and physical therapists; and care administration, which consists of all administrative information about the patient, such as referral handling, time booking, and registration.

During our first attempt to introduce the system in one PHC we faced the following problems:

1. Absence of knowledge and skills to use the new system

2. Unwillingness to adapt to the new system

3. Suboptimal human-computer interaction

The lack of knowledge and skills was reported by the end-users of the system as a direct consequence of inadequate training before the system was implemented. Practitioners in general found that they did not have enough time to train before "having to do it in reality." Nurses and other non-physician staff were particularly dissatisfied, because they thought that the training sessions were based mostly on physicians' needs.

The users also indicated that once the system went live, ongoing support was reported to be inadequate for the success of the newly implemented system. The users wanted ongoing help in order to overcome day-to-day problems.

The human-computer interaction had several technical shortcomings that remained after the implementation of the integrated system. The login process was found to be time consuming. Several features were perceived to be less than user-friendly, causing dissatisfaction and discord. Requesting a specific file consumed more time than in the previous system. The integrated system also required use of new terms, concepts, and connotations, and the users emphasized that learning this information took time.

The fact that the new system changed current workflows occasioned an unwillingness to adapt to the new system in use. The clinical personnel expressed dissatisfaction and criticism. The respondents also made complaints about the short timeframe for the implementation at the pilot site. They believed that the decision makers implemented the system too quickly, which caused many educational problems, mainly learning terms and navigation routines. Users questioned whether there was a strong foundation prior to implementation, including adequate staff and financial resources.

Author's Analysis

Because of the high costs associated with EHRs, organizations need to have a long-term financial plan and understand the total cost of EHRs. Based on user expectations and attitudes, greater user involvement during the design and implementation phase of the system would provide better insight into existing workflows and work practices. From the users' point of view, this would have helped define the system requirements in more detail and revise work practices to better integrate the new system.

The results of this attempted EHR implementation show that one of the most important factors that influence the outcome of integrated EHR implementation is the design of the user training program. Our users' experience of being unable to manage interaction with the new system caused secondary issues, such as the opinion that the integrated EHR was not appropriately designed. Further, it seems to be necessary to stimulate close coordination of operations where the clinical and the informatics groups work together.

The consequences of this process suggest that medical informaticians must learn from the past in order to communicate and adapt our own practices based on experience and research. However, an alternative explanation of the findings is that the unsatisfactory situation was caused by traditionally structured educational programs that were used with a new generation of technologies and end-users. Compared to a decade ago, end-users currently have more experience using computers, which means that requests and preferences should be considered. It may therefore be a mistake to believe that the training task is finished when a clinician has undergone initial training and is using the EHR. Ongoing and continued education and training may be necessary to optimize clinician efficiency and effectiveness.

How to solve the remaining technical issues is therefore not the only question when continuing the implementation of the integrated EHR. In fact, perhaps the most important question concerns how the implementation process can be adapted to meet different professional needs.

Previous evaluation studies have shown that the implementation process of a new EHR is an expensive activity. Evaluations of EHR implementations have often shown limited success, and they have failed to consistently demonstrate improvements in patient care, operating costs savings, and improvements in productivity. This study shows that we have in fact not learned from the past. The same results have been reported by hundreds of other evaluators. It seems therefore that before we continue to use the scarce resources available in healthcare organizations, it is necessary to develop strategies to involve end-users of the new system and ask them for help to accelerate organizational change as well as work routines.

Acceptance of planned change seems to be fundamental for success. Decision makers in the future should therefore plan to expedite the social process of trial and error in order to help organizations develop the necessary changes that match new technology or innovations to facilitate and accelerate the benefits that innovations have the potential to produce.

Editor's Commentary (L. Ozeran, MD)

The authors of this story are aware of this common process failure, and yet they did it anyway (or perhaps the health system's management did). Is your organization aware and still implementing the same wrong processes? If you want to save time and money, stop repeating the well-known mistakes of others! Every editor on this book has seen this process failure at least once.

You have a choice: You can ignore the needs of your users and implement what you think they need, what you want them to have, the cheapest available solution, or any number of wrong answers.

Conversely, you can work with your users. This often costs more up front and takes longer to implement, but it is cheaper in the long run and the only way to obtain a functional system.

1. The short version of what works is:

2. Ensure all stakeholders are involved in the HIT selection process either directly, if your organization is small, or indirectly through representatives who have similar roles. When stakeholders are to be represented, let the stakeholders choose their representative to ensure that this person is someone who the stakeholders respect and to whom they will be comfortable presenting their perspectives. During the process, ensure that bidirectional communication is occurring—that the representatives are both sending progress reports back to their constituents and that perspectives of the constituents are being presented. This may require periodically

checking in with random stakeholders who are not representatives to be certain that this communication is actually occurring.

3. Document existing workflows and how they might change under a new system. Perform a gap analysis, determining the difference between where you are and where you would like to be. Educate stakeholders about what is possible, what is affordable, and what is likely. Obtain adequate input about stakeholder priorities to ensure that the highest priorities are implemented and be prepared to explain why other priorities cannot be implemented or when they might be implemented in the future. Minimize changes to workflow.

4. Plan adequately for the implementation and training. Ensure that there is adequate staff for the expected productivity loss or, if possible in your environment, decrease the workload. Ensure that trainers are present and readily available on site initially and by phone or on call once the system seems to be working well. The decision as to whether the system is working well must be made by the users. Provide training in a learning laboratory prior to implementation if you want to reduce real-time errors. Evaluate all participants with a standardized series of tasks before graduating them from the learning laboratory.

5. When possible, implement in phases. Lessons learned from initial implementations may then be used during subsequent phases. If you plan adequately for a phased implementation, you may be able to negotiate lower initial costs that ramp up only as you add active users. You may also need fewer extra staff to manage the initial productivity hit.

6. Include RFIs and RFPs received from your vendor as addenda in your contract to ensure the vendor meets all of their verbal commitments. Ensure that you contract for adequate training and support—this is often underestimated or underbudgeted. If you want to reduce vendor problems, include specific but reasonable penalties for noncompliance. If timelines are included, there should be clear penalties for delays.

Remember that the fastest and easiest way to go forward is for the CIO to choose the systems and implement them with no input. If you are choosing an easy path in implementing your EHR, you are probably doing it wrong. It's your choice. Choose wisely.

Lessons Learned

- Involve clinicians in the project strategy and plan.
- Involve clinicians in the product selection process.
- Involve clinicians in the implementation and management.
- Communicate effectively across all involved disciplines throughout the project life cycle.
- Effective change management and training are essential for successful EHR projects.

Chapter 15

Failure to Scale

═══════════════════════════════════════

A PDA-Based Teaching Module

Editor: G. Keenan, PhD, RN

Key Words: ambulatory electronic health record (EHR), documentation, medical education, student, testing, user interface

Project Categories: infrastructure and technology

Lessons Learned Categories: technology problems

Case Study

═══════════════════════════════════════

Students at our institution have read-access to numerous clinical electronic record systems, but none of these specifically augment medical education. Students' electronic data-recording opportunities are almost nonexistent. For several years we have developed student patient record (SPR) programs that record a small amount of information about students' clinical encounters. These modest contents have provided educational decision support and summary statistics in primary care settings. We attempted to expand SPR use to all third-year clinical rotations.

SPR version 5 was a stable program built in Satellite Forms 5 and tailored to loaned Palm Tungsten C handheld devices. For new patients, students could record demographics, then record diagnoses arranged by patient type, often using one tap per diagnosis, without scrolling or typing. Family Medicine's new patient types were distinguished by age: Adult, Teen, Child, Infant, and Baby. In SPR 5, students recorded 70% of ambulatory care diagnoses from new patient screens, and could find additional diagnoses in shallow tree structures or alphabetized lists.

Students received small rewards for thorough, statistically plausible documentation.

We encountered a serious limitation in the design environment while expanding the number of screens representing diagnoses as check boxes in SPR 6: Satellite Forms 6 was recompiling the global script anew for every check box, causing extremely long compile times. We were forced to remove the reminder system from the global script while waiting for the new Satellite Forms vendor to repair the problem in version 7. Every student was loaned a Tungsten E2 computer. These affordable handheld devices proved at least three times slower than the Tungsten C when opening SPR or filtering long lists.

We had no wireless network. Students sometimes compromised data gathering by changing key user identification, declining to install a critical update, or ignoring the program completely. We generally had to detect and react to these events in person.

Other clerkships wanted students to document completion of explicit goals rather than complete patients. Although much of the SPR 5 interface was faster than paper for recording diagnoses in primary care settings, and all goals were represented similarly in SPR 6, goals were not actually listed or tracked. Furthermore, students changed clinical settings approximately every 4 weeks, so they regularly had to learn new button arrangements tailored to new courses. Course directors voiced concerns that students were spending more time on documentation than seeing patients.

We had relied on infrared beaming and regular contact with small numbers of students to collect data from SPR 5. Several clerkships had intermittent contact with large groups of students using SPR 6. Infrared beaming was extremely cumbersome in these circumstances.

A Web-based status report was the only verification that a student had met course goals. We had only 0.4 FTE divided between two individuals to develop and maintain SPR 6, a server, and the reporting programs. Personal distractions delayed the delivery of the reporting system. When reports became available, some additional goal documentation and data collecting problems were exposed. Efforts to appease frustrated students included suspending SPR documentation and allowing them to purchase the Tungsten E2s at a discount.

SPR 7 attempted to address all SPR 6 problems with the exception of wireless networking. SPR 7 disposed of button arrays and added security, dynamic list management, goal tracking and goal-based documentation, decision support, dynamic input area support, and interactive help features. The SPR 7 interface was tailored to the fastest affordable and available Palm device, the TX, running the new nonvolatile file system and the Garnet 5.4.9 operating system (OS).

We sought speed enhancements using extensions to Satellite Forms 7. Late in testing we discovered situations causing SPR 7 to crash with a cache error on the TX. This seemed to occur when extensions encountered boundary conditions. Cache errors were malignant. After suffering one crash on a TX, SPR 7 crashed at progressively earlier steps, quickly becoming useless. One day before scheduled deployment we found more cache errors and could not correct these in the ensuing week. Our Palm-based project was canceled.

Author's Analysis

We experienced numerous difficulties with SPR 6 and 7, nearly all related to scaling a previously successful project in a narrow domain to more courses, more simultaneous student users, and more administrators' needs. Some key points are:

- Participant's goals need to be reconciled or managed proactively. Most of our institution was interested in goal tracking whereas we saw much more promise in demonstrating the benefits of more thorough, patient-oriented documentation. We are rebuilding SPR for Windows Mobile with our attention directed first to meeting the documentation needs of administrators. From the student perspective, deploying SPR 6 without the reminder system scuttled the last reason we could offer for thorough documentation.

- An interface that works when learned once may not work when users must relearn it often. If the interface content changes, it should provide some other consistency, such as alphabetized or structured lists. We emphasize that this lesson may not apply to practicing physicians. The diminutive SPR 5/6 interface is faster than paper for recording 70% of students' primary care diagnoses when they are graded on completeness. If a user consistently works in a domain having predictable clusters of recordable concepts, then similar interfaces may be optimal.

- Adequate resource allocations are essential. Wireless or Internet-based services are almost indispensable for deploying updates and collecting data from many users. Important projects require more developer depth and redundancy than we had.

- Early and aggressive testing on the target platform is invaluable. Hardware and operating system changes can interact badly with software tools. Although we waited more than 1 year from its first release to use the TX and Garnet 5.4.9, and thought that our development tools were stable on the new platform, we were wrong.

Editor's Commentary (G. Keenan, PhD, RN)

This story is an example of what many others have experienced when there is insufficient planning before the development of information technology (IT). Although the story does not describe the initial SPR development phase, it seems apparent that proper planning could have produced better outcomes. As the field of IT grows in healthcare, the importance of planning and sufficient testing cannot be overstated. Abandoning a technology that was not built to scale fuels increases in the already out-of-control healthcare costs with the corresponding adverse implications for patients, clinicians, and organizations.

Indeed, it is nearly impossible to isolate all of the hardware, software, user, content, and political factors that might influence how an application will be used across time. It is also outlandish to focus on meeting only the immediate needs of the user without attention to the reality that user needs naturally grow and change across time. Our team has managed to avoid early obsolescence with our IT innovations by keeping a 10-year development plan current. We carefully envision and create plans about what we want based on what we think is possible in 10 years, adjusting the plan each year. As we have found, creating a plan to sustain an IT innovation for a decade has forced us to create a flexible product that can readily handle multiple types of contingencies both known and unknown. Of course there will always be some costs associated with evolving a product over time; however, we believe vigilant and creative long-term planning are key to keeping overall costs to a minimum.

Lessons Learned

- Considering the long-term possibilities of an IT innovation prior to development ensures the product can grow and scale with minimal costs, including changes in hardware, software, policy, user, and content.

- Adequate testing with all types of users under the conditions of use is essential for evaluating the true value of any IT innovation.
- Seeking input of users, although essential, is insufficient to build successful IT innovations.
  - A solid ongoing collaborative partnership between technical and clinical experts is equally as important.
- Project planning should be an ongoing aspect of any HIT initiative, with governance document changes as necessary.

Chapter 16

"Meaningful Use"?

A Small Practice EHR

Editor: L. Ozeran, MD

Key Words: charge capture, decision support, efficiency, electronic health record (EHR), meaningful use, quality improvement, solo practice, training

Project Categories: ambulatory electronic health record (EHR)

Lessons Learned Categories: system design, technology problems, training

Case Study

A young primary care physician, after practicing for several years at the same urban community health center where he had undergone residency training, decided it was time for a change. Despite having had no experience in either solo private practice or in the use of EHR systems, he decided to establish his own solo practice and to use an EHR system from the first day, with no paper records. The decision to purchase and install an EHR system required a substantial capital investment and was a highly unusual step for a solo, private-practice physician in that city (itself a rare breed there).

The physician cited two main factors in the decision to adopt an EHR: efficiency and effective charge capture. "I wanted to be able to get my [visit] notes done quickly and bill electronically, and also not have the overhead for storage of paper charts." He also cited quality and patient-safety benefits such as drug-drug interaction warnings offered when using the EHR to generate prescriptions, and reminders regarding preventive interventions for which the patient is due. The initial installation and configuration of the EHR was uneventful, and the physician and staff received training from the EHR vendor at the time of initial installation.

Over several years, the practice grew to three physicians and two midlevel practitioners. A physician with some informatics training joined the practice. The new physician made some noteworthy observations:

- Although newer versions of the EHR system were available, the practice continued to use the version that was current when the practice was founded years before.

- Some processes (such as generating outside referrals) were being handled with paper, despite the capability of the EHR to handle them electronically.

- Certain configurable content, such as the rules on which automated reminders regarding preventive care are based, had not been changed since being automatically set during the initial software installation, despite changes in the evidence-based standards of care on which they were based.

- Certain basic security practices—such as assigning each user a separate user account and not sharing passwords—were not being followed .

- Many of the features of the software, some among them frequently cited as conferring the most important benefits of an EHR, were being used rarely or not at all: e-prescribing and computerized provider order entry (CPOE), assignment of discrete codes to patient diagnoses and problems, population-based reporting tools, creation of custom data fields to record discrete data of interest, and customization of documentation templates.

When these observations were pointed out to the practice's founding physician, he thought that although true, these observations were not of serious concern. "The program is effective for what I need it to do. I realize it can do a lot more, but I'm pretty happy with what I get out of it now, and I don't really have the time to get into all the details" of utilizing features such as those just mentioned. However, he acknowledged the potential value of such functionality, particularly in promoting patient safety and improving quality:

I realize that a lot of the quality experts want us to use EHRs to do patient recalls, population-based care, and quality measurement . . . and I want to do all that too. I think sometimes what the experts don't realize is that physicians, particularly those in private practice, where we're responsible for everything, need help just getting through the day taking care of our patients, and we focus on the aspects of an EHR that let us do that. I hope we can get to the rest of it someday soon.

Recently, the practice started taking steps to get more out of their EHR. They have upgraded to the latest version, started using the EHR's electronic prescribing capability (that is, electronic transmission of prescriptions directly to pharmacies, rather than printing or faxing prescriptions from the EHR), and are planning on participating in a quality improvement initiative that will provide reports on key quality measures extracted from data in their EHR. The growth of the practice to its current five providers has increased the level of product knowledge among the providers, as each gradually (often accidentally) discovers new aspects of how the EHR can be used and shares it with the others.

Author's Analysis

The case history raises the question of what "failure" means in the adoption and use of HIT. Specifically, this case illustrates that there are gradations of failure short of complete abandonment or deinstallation of a system, and that failure is, in some cases, a matter of context or expectations. The practice's founding physician absolutely does not see the practice's use of an EHR as a "failure." Quite to the contrary, the specific goals in mind when the decision to use an EHR was made, to allow documenting care more quickly than on paper without the expense of a transcriptionist; to avoid the space and associated expenses entailed by paper records, and to minimize accounts receivable through electronic claims submission, by any analysis were met.

On the other hand, many "experts" in clinical informatics and clinical quality improvement, blanching at the thought of the most valuable (from their perspective) features of an EHR going underused or unused, would look on this case history as a failure to obtain the maximum benefit from an EHR (Zhou et al. 2009). There are few published data on the frequency with which specific features of ambulatory EHRs are actually utilized (Simon et al. 2009). However, abundant anecdotal experience suggests that the case study is not unusual, and this might explain recently published data suggesting that use of an EHR alone is not associated with quality of care.

Practicing physicians and the experts do agree on one thing: the quality benefits obtained through capture and storage of discrete data in the EHR and leveraging of that data for just-in-time decision support and population-level care management are significant and worth striving toward. The question of "failure" in this case, then, becomes a simple matter of perspective on the pace of this evolution of the healthcare process. However, challenging questions remain: How can EHRs be engineered so that these more "advanced" features are easier to use? How can the organization of healthcare services and their financing be restructured to increase the feasibility of more effective utilization of EHR technology? How can physicians, particularly busy ones trying to run a practice on their own and who may need training and assistance, be identified, and how can that training and assistance be provided to them?

Editor's Commentary (L. Ozeran, MD, and J. Leviss, MD)

The author's final questions are particularly important since the passage of the American Recovery and Reinvestment Act of 2009 (ARRA). Under the ARRA, the United States federal government committed approximately $20 billion to HIT initiatives, including billions for payment incentives for physicians to use EHRs in a manner that provides "meaningful use." As this book goes to print, the exact definition of, or requirements for, "meaningful use" are being debated by every U.S. healthcare, healthcare technology, and healthcare informatics organization; the U.S. Office of the National Coordinator for Health IT (ONC), under the Department of Health and Human Services, will ultimately clarify the definition of "meaningful use," and, in effect, add commentary to cases such as the one described herein.

Regarding the assessment of this case study, it might be instructive to know how much the physician paid for the system and support services as a percentage of revenues. Similarly, it might be useful to know how many patients the physician was seeing and how many hours were spent in the clinic each day compared to after being in solo practice for 1 year. This would provide more concrete evidence that the system was, in fact, a success for the goals the physician initially set.

The bigger issue, as the author has accurately noted, is how this scenario plays across the country, which has implications for our entire nation's healthcare system. As physicians and informaticists, we usually have two primary goals for EHRs: better care and lower costs. If we can provide the best care at the right time, we can likely achieve our goals. If decision support relies on old data or is not considered, both the nation's healthcare system and the patient lose. Unfortunately, all EHRs require training, and training requires time and resources. Most physicians currently feel overwhelmed by the amount of clinical and administrative work they must complete and often feel underpaid for their efforts. This is not a situation that encourages individuals to dedicate time without compensation to benefit the nation's health system, even if a quality of care 'moral imperative' advocates such efforts. The next few years will demonstrate whether the ARRA affects this pattern and whether "meaningful use" was attained by this practice or even is attainable by small physician practices in the US.

Lessons Learned

- A successful EHR meets the needs of the practice.
- EHR functionality may go unused or underutilized if the cost to implement appears to be greater than the benefit.
- Training requires a time commitment that must be seen as worthwhile to the trainee.
- EHR features that may benefit the healthcare system in aggregate may not be a priority for busy physicians who do not see the benefit as worth the cost.
- Increasing use of underused EHR features may require an easier user interface, repair of our healthcare system, or direct compensation to physicians for use.

Chapter 17

104 Synergistic Problems

An Enterprise EHR

Editor: E. Rose, MD

Key Words: electronic health record (EHR), downtime, end-user involvement, sociotechnical issues, vendor contracts, workflow

Project Categories: inpatient electronic health record (EHR)

Lessons Learned Categories: leadership, project management, technology problems, workflow

Case Study

This HIT story describes an implementation of an integrated EHR system in a large university teaching hospital. The project started in 2001 and the implementation progressed slowly from one hospital unit to the next. The main parts of the system were *Orfeus,* for controlling and administrating healthcare processes and *Medeia,* for recording the care planning, realization, follow-up, and evaluation. The software provider had missed delivery dates and the parts delivered had not always met the original specifications. These challenges, combined with technical and integration problems, caused resistance among the hospital staff.

The resistance peaked in the surgical outpatient clinic and surgical inpatient unit where our story took place. The implementation was carried out in two of the surgical units during November 2005, but the situation was soon called a crisis by the staff members and the implementation came to a halt. In order to restart the project successfully, an assessment was performed to identify problems and recommend potential solutions. When studying the situation's problems, we interviewed surgeons, nurses, administration, and other EHR project stakeholders and identified 104 different issues of concern. These issues were classified into first-, second-, and third-order groups after the issue order model presented by Star and Ruhleder (1996).

First-order issues:

First-order issues are often easily visible and solutions to them are practical. These issues were grouped according to the themes of redistribution of work resources and working time, arranging user training, and in relation to technical problems during the implementation.

After the implementation of the EHR, a main issue in information access was caused by workflows that were impeded. The process to use the EHR was slower than using the paper records at hand. One of the system features that increased slowness was the structured character of the EHR. For example, there were more than 50 headings for recording a nursing action. One of the nurses described the situation as follows:

Now I have to open *Medeia,* to open the nursing records. Now I'll create the record, that takes many clicks—like surgeons' names, date, and cause this and cause that. Then I'll have to choose the right headings, and then I can go and record the day visit by the patient . . . and then I'll have to choose the next suitable heading... I have many workflow steps here, steps that I have never done before . . . Before I just wrote, for example, 'covering letter' and 'breast cancer' on the paper and that was it.

The slowness of use affected workflows in various ways. For example, in the surgical outpatient department with continuous patient visits, half of the working time consists of documenting patient records. In contrast, this took only about one eighth of the working time in the surgical inpatient unit.

Second-order issues:

Second-order issues can be caused by unpredictable contextual effects; that is, a collision or combination of two or more first-order issues. The unexpected effects may be caused by technical choices made or by the differences between the various cultures of practice that are working together in the implementation.

Combined effects of technical features that caused user resistance were, for example, the way the EHR logged off users, how the technical devices were arranged in the inpatient areas, or other problems that might have been caused by a constant need to repeat login to the system. Constant technical problems caused the staff to think that the EHR did not ease their documenting load but rather interfered with their work-flow and caused unwanted periods of waiting for the system to open or to find the next patient's data. Technical problems were further illustrated by the varied practices during downtime of the EHR system. During downtime, the patient records could be written as separate text files that could then be added into the EHR when the system was up again. Problems emerged when the separate text files were attached only as printouts to the paper version of the patient records and not into the EHR. The result was that the EHR was not necessarily up to date, and that the staff could not trust the information in the EHR as complete or accurate.

Third-order issues:

Third-order issues are often political or social by nature. Their nature dictates that these problems are also hard to solve. Such problems can be caused by the historical reasons behind the choices made in the imple-mentation project or distinct features in the organizational culture.

The staff in the surgical clinic thought that they had no influence in the system design and development. While working bedside, both a surgeon and a nurse might record information quite fluently and not consider whose user account was used to access the system. Problems of responsibility emerged when mistakes were made in the records. The one whose username was logged into the system was held responsible. On the other hand, surgeons feared that the slowness of use could cause malpractice in situations when patient information could not be accessed as easily as needed. A surgeon might have had to make a decision on patient care with insufficient information.

Author's Analysis

The conflicting situation was caused by a combination of multiple and intertwined sociotechnical issues. Emergence of such issues demanded attention on several levels in the organization, in this case, for example, by the information management department and hospital administra-tion. The preliminary results suggest that social structures affecting the interaction in a hospital unit affect how the emergence of intertwined problems, handling the issues, and resolving the crisis takes place.

With previous manual patient records, the staff members were used to interpreting the paper records. Now with the EHR, the feelings of insecurity emerged as well as the fear of ignorance as the previously usable interpretive schemes were insufficient in the changing context of interpretation. With the EHR, the patient information was "hidden" behind different headings of new nursing classifications and behind the views in the new system environment. Furthermore, the EHR was designed as independent system components. These components can work quite well by themselves, but the integration had caused some unexpected effects. Uncertainty combined with technical problems caused user resistance to reach its peak, and thus the implementation and use of the EHR came to a halt.

The case study shows that a new, unfamiliar information system can be accused of shortcomings or problems that may not actually be caused by the technology. In a crisis situation it is a human reaction to find a "scapegoat" that can be accused. Instead of simply labeling the new information system as a "scapegoat," we want to ask whether the implementation of an information system is a catalyst that makes it possible for other sociotechnical issues to emerge in the organizational context. The case study indicates that technical problems, such as slowness of use, can cause user resistance or at least increase users' doubt about the new information system. On the other hand, issues concerning professional values, such as fear of malpractice because of missing or inaccessible patient information, can lead to the decision not to use the system at all.

Editor's Commentary (E. Rose, MD)

This fascinating case history of a HIT project that went seriously awry offers a smorgasbord of cautionary points. As the title suggests, it seems that every possible mishap that can occur in such a project took place.

It would be interesting to know what the decision-making process was for selecting the system used and its configuration. It seems likely, given the outcome, that involvement of the end users—at least from the surgery department—was minimal. If there had been such end-user involvement, the usability issues described herein would likely have been recognized even before the purchasing decision was made, and/or the system would probably have been tailored to more closely match the true needs of the clinical staff.

The references to "slipped schedules" and the vendor-supplied software "not always meeting specifications" points to the importance of careful negotiation of vendor contracts. Such happenstances are not uncommon, and often are unavoidable (to be fair to the vendors), and this serves to underscore that organizations relying on vendor-supplied software should ensure that purchasing contracts clearly stipulate what remedies will be offered in such circumstances, and also include contingencies in their implementation plan for them.

The "issue order model" used to group the problems encountered in this project helps to differentiate problems that are straightforward and practical (though not necessarily easily solved) from those that involve interactions among several factors, such as the issue with adding the text files, which were created during periods of downtime, back to the EHR. This latter issue requires a consistent workflow outside the use of the EHR, which is often hard to achieve. The "third order" issues in this case history describe interactions between the EHR system's characteristics and the professional realities of medical practice colliding and serve to remind us of the high stakes where the safety of real patients, and the professional standing of real healthcare practitioners, are involved.

Lessons Learned

- Stakeholder involvement in project planning and technology selection is critical.
- Technology-driven workflows must fit the needs of clinicians.
- Costs of project delays to both health systems and vendors should be reviewed prior to a technology implementation.
- HIT initiatives exist within the complex sociopolitical culture of the healthcare delivery system and are influenced positively and negatively by the organizations involved.

Part III

Conclusion

Chapter 18

Conclusion— A Review of HIT Failure

*S. Silverstein, MD, B. Kaplan, PhD,
L. Ozeran, MD, and J. Leviss, MD*

The major purpose of this book is to share wisdom with the professionals tasked with the responsibilities for designing, implementing, and managing HIT so they may be successful with their HIT endeavors. The storytelling format is intended to make it easier for readers to reach out to peers, superiors, and subordinates to say "this could be us." The goal is to educate everyone involved in the process about the social and organizational issues affecting this sector in addition to the technical challenges, to help people learn from the past, and to avoid known errors that have already caused project problems and failures. Knowledge about people, organizations, implementation, and maintenance issues has grown over the years, both within medical informatics itself and through contributions from other disciplines (Ash et al. 2008; Kaplan and Shaw 2004). There is an emerging consensus that problems are caused by social, cultural, and financial issues, and hence, are more managerial than technical (Kaplan and Harris-Salamone 2009).

Clinical information technology (IT) projects are highly complex social endeavors in unforgiving medical environments that happen to involve computers, not IT projects that happen to involve clinicians. If you have read only a few of the stories in this book, this should be very clear to you. Having presented you with the realities of HIT in the institution, we wanted to close by introducing you to some of the theory, which is still early in development but offers a theoretical framework that is both practical and well grounded in research(Kaplan 2001a).

Although there are many useful theories and frameworks (Kaplan and Shaw 2004), two are popular among informaticians analyzing the kinds of issues that our case studies illustrate. One is Roger's Diffusion of Innovation (Rogers 2003) and its extensions to address gaps relevant to HIT implementations (Lorenzi et al. 2008). Another is sociotechnical theory (Harrison et al. 2007). Both are social interactionist theories (Kaplan 2001b). Social interactionist theories in informatics were developed and extended by the late Rob Kling, the father of social informatics (SI), during his tenure at the University of California-Irvine, and then at Indiana University. This book should give the study of HIT difficulties, a social informatics endeavor, increased visibility and respectability among the medical informatics community.

Kling thought that many information and communications technology (ICT) professionals have an inadequate understanding of ICT, the actions and interactions of people who use them, and the organizational and social contexts in which they are used. Social informatics refers to the interdisciplinary study of the design, uses, and consequences of ICTs that takes into account their interaction with institutional and cultural realities. Kling also recommended that communicating SI research to others is important because the value of SI theory, insights, and findings has relevance across a range of disciplines. He defines a major challenge in drawing SI work together and beginning to make it known to other academic communities (Kling and Rosenbaum 2005, 107–108).

The principles of SI can be summarized as:

1. The context of ICT use directly affects its meaning and roles.

2. ICTs are not "value neutral"—they create winners and losers.

3. The effects of ICT use leads to multiple and often paradoxical effects that are multifarious and unpredictable.

4. ICT use has ethical aspects.

5. ICTs are configurable.

6. ICTs follow trajectories, often favoring the status quo.

7. ICTs coevolve before and after implementation; all are social activities.

Most important of all is critical thinking about ICT projects; that is, developing the ability to examine ICTs from perspectives that do not automatically and implicitly adopt the goals and beliefs of the groups that commission, design, or implement specific ICTs. Critical thinking also entails developing an ability to reflect on issues at a number of levels and from more than one perspective (Kling et al. 2000, 123). For these reasons, according to Marc Berg, one of sociotechnical theory's main expositors, the idea of "success factors" becomes problematic, as they entail the idea that a fixed list of activities and characteristics will ensure "success." "Success" depends both on the point of view of users who may differ in whether and to what degree they consider a system "successful," and on the specific situation and the complex processes of addressing the kinds of insights Kling identified (Berg 2001).

These principles explain why Kaplan's review of individual, organizational, and social issues identified the fit of information and communication technologies with other contextual issues surrounding their development, implementation, and use as crucial to their success. Research on these principles include the importance of fit with:

- Workflow and routines
- Clinicians' level of expertise
- Values and professional norms
- Institutional setting, history, and structure
- Communication patterns, organizational culture, status relationships, control relationships, division of labor, work roles, and professional responsibility
- Cognitive processes
- Congruence with existing organizational business models and strategic partners
- Compatibility with clinical patient encounter and consultation patterns
- The extent to which models embodied in a system are shared by its users

Authors have also addressed (in various ways) fit between information technology and how individuals define their work, user characteristics, and preferences (for example, information needs), the clinical operating model under which a system is used, and the organization into which it is introduced. Others have focused on interrelationships among key components of an organization, (for example, organizational structure, strategy, management, people's skills, and technology) and compatibility of goals, professional values, needs, and cultures of different groups within an organization, including developers, clinicians, administrators, and patients. In addition, studies have been done on ways in which informatics applications embody values, norms, representations of work and work routines, assumptions about usability, information content and style of presentation, and links between medical knowledge and clinical practice; and how these assumptions influence system design (Kaplan and Shaw 2004; Kaplan 2001b).

Kaplan's research also identified the same four barriers—insufficient funding, technology, and knowledge; poor project management; the organization of medicine and healthcare; and physician resistance—blamed for lack of diffusion of ICT in healthcare since the 1950s. These barriers are characterized by looking to external causes for the problems in our field (Kaplan 1987). They are evidence of beliefs Kling and Iaconno characterized as computerization movements that too often characterize the driving forces behind clinical IT (Kling and Iaconno 1988). Among these beliefs is the technologically deterministic view that ICT in and of itself, not SI principles, will cause organizational and individual change in healthcare delivery and the practice of medicine. A close relative of technological determinism is the "*magic bullet*" theory, where people believe they are change agents if they initiate or develop IT because they think IT itself has the power to create organizational change. These people describe IT as a "*magic bullet*" and believe that they have built the gun (Markus and Benjamin 1997). Unfamiliarity with the findings of SI research and beliefs in technologic determinism directly contribute to healthcare IT failure.

Some authors in the healthcare informatics sphere have begun to challenge the dominant paradigm (Koppel et al. 2005; Han et al. 2005), but not without raising significant controversy and receiving considerable criticism, (despite significant problems in local and national EHR initiatives in the United States and abroad (Freudenheim 2004; Peel and Rose 2009). Yet there is interest in information on HIT difficulties and a snapshot of this interest was gauged via analysis of Web access logs to a Website on HIT failure (Silverstein 2006).

This book is also meant to serve as a tool to show that this inquiry is both valuable and respectable, and to start meeting the need for practical information on how to increase chances for project success. Assessments of failures must continue and the lessons learned must be shared broadly if we are to meet the call to leverage HIT to dramatically improve health systems across the U.S. and the world.

Next steps for readers could include:

- Review existing and upcoming projects for failure risk factors identified in the cases of this book and address them
- Incorporate lessons learned into standard project strategies and plans to maximize project success rates
- Collaborate on regional exchanges of lessons learned from failed initiatives at conferences, virtually, and/or via printed communications, to continue to develop resources and guides that help projects succeed

Although those who fail to learn from history are doomed to repeat its mistakes, those who learn from the wisdom of those who've *"been there"* will prosper.

Part IV
Appendixes

Appendix A

Project and Lessons Learned Categories

Project Categories

Ambulatory Electronic Health Record (EHR)

- Chapter 11: Leadership and Strategy
- Chapter 12: Designing Custom Software for Quality Reports
- Chapter 14: Clinician Adoption
- Chapter 16: "Meaningful Use"?
- Chapter 17: 104 Synergistic Problems

Inpatient Electronic Health Record (EHR)

- Chapter 1: Build It with Them, Make It Mandatory, and They Will Come
- Chapter 2: Hospital Objectives vs. Project Timelines
- Chapter 3: Clinical Quality Improvement or Administrative Oversight
- Chapter 5: Basic Math
- Chapter 6: Technological Iatrogenesis from "Downtime"
- Chapter 7: Trained as Planned
- Chapter 9: If It Ain't Broke, Don't Fix It
- Chapter 10: Effective Leadership Includes the Right People
- Chapter 13: If It's Designed and Built by One, It Will Not Serve the Needs of Many

Computerized Provider Order Entry (CPOE)

- Chapter 1: Build It with Them, Make It Mandatory, and They Will Come
- Chapter 3: Clinical Quality Improvement or Administrative Oversight
- Chapter 5: Basic Math
- Chapter 14: Clinician Adoption

Electronic Medication Administration Record (eMAR)

- Chapter 2: Hospital Objectives vs. Project Timelines
- Chapter 5: Basic Math
- Chapter 6: Technological Iatrogenesis from "Downtime"

Pharmacy IS

- Chapter 5: Basic Math
- Chapter 6: Technological Iatrogenesis from "Downtime"

Infrastructure and Technology

- Chapter 4: A Single Point of Failure
- Chapter 8: Device Selection—No Other Phase Is More Important
- Chapter 15: Failure to Scale

Lessons Learned Categories

Communication

- Chapter 2: Hospital Objectives vs. Project Timelines
- Chapter 3: Clinical Quality Improvement or Administrative Oversight
- Chapter 6: Technological Iatrogenesis from "Downtime"
- Chapter 7: Trained as Planned
- Chapter 14: Clinician Adoption

Contracts

- Chapter 6: Technological Iatrogenesis from "Downtime"
- Chapter 17: 104 Synergistic Problems

Data Model
- Chapter 10: Effective Leadership Includes the Right People
- Chapter 12: Designing Custom Software for Quality Reports

Implementation Approaches
- Chapter 1: Build It with Them, Make It Mandatory, and They Will Come

Leadership
- Chapter 1: Build It with Them, Make It Mandatory, and They Will Come
- Chapter 2: Hospital Objectives vs. Project Timelines
- Chapter 6: Technological Iatrogenesis from "Downtime"
- Chapter 7: Trained as Planned
- Chapter 8: Device Selection—No Other Phase Is More Important
- Chapter 9: If It Ain't Broke, Don't Fix It
- Chapter 10: Effective Leadership Includes the Right People
- Chapter 11: Leadership and Strategy
- Chapter 13: If It's Designed and Built by One, It Will Not Serve the Needs of Many
- Chapter 14: Clinician Adoption
- Chapter 17: 104 Synergistic Problems

Project Management
- Chapter 4: A Single Point of Failure
- Chapter 7: Trained as Planned
- Chapter 8: Device Selection—No Other Phase Is More Important
- Chapter 11: Leadership and Strategy
- Chapter 12: Designing Custom Software for Quality Reports
- Chapter 17: 104 Synergistic Problems

Staffing Resources
- Chapter 2: Hospital Objectives vs. Project Timelines
- Chapter 6: Technological Iatrogenesis from "Downtime"
- Chapter 7: Trained as Planned
- Chapter 11: Leadership and Strategy

- Chapter 13: If It's Designed and Built by One, It Will Not Serve the Needs of Many

System Configuration
- Chapter 5: Basic Math
- Chapter 10: Effective Leadership Includes the Right People

System Design
- Chapter 9: If It Ain't Broke, Don't Fix It
- Chapter 16: "Meaningful Use"?

Technology Problems
- Chapter 4: A Single Point of Failure
- Chapter 2: Hospital Objectives vs. Project Timelines
- Chapter 5: Basic Math
- Chapter 6: Technological Iatrogenesis from "Downtime"
- Chapter 14: Clinician Adoption
- Chapter 15: Failure to Scale
- Chapter 16: "Meaningful Use"?
- Chapter 17: 104 Synergistic Problems

Training
- Chapter 6: Technological Iatrogenesis from "Downtime"
- Chapter 7: Trained as Planned
- Chapter 14: Clinician Adoption
- Chapter 16: "Meaningful Use"?

Workflow
- Chapter 3: Clinical Quality Improvement or Administrative Oversight
- Chapter 8: Device Selection—No Other Phase Is More Important
- Chapter 9: If It Ain't Broke, Don't Fix It
- Chapter 13: If It's Designed and Built by One, It Will Not Serve the Needs of Many
- Chapter 14: Clinician Adoption
- Chapter 17: 104 Synergistic Problems

Appendix B

Text References and Bibliography of Additional Resources

Text References

Ash, J.S., N.R. Anderson, and P. Tarczy-Hornoch. 2008. People and organizational issues in research systems implementation. *Journal of the American Medical Informatics Association* 15(3):283-289.

Bakken, S. 2001. An informatics infrastructure is essential for evidence-based practice. *Journal of the American Medical Informatics Association* 8:199-201.

Berg, M. 2001. Implementing information systems in health care organizations: myths and challenges. *International Journal of Medical Informatics* 64:143-156.

Freudenheim, M. 2004 (April 6). Many hospitals resist computerized patient care. *New York Times.* http://www.nytimes.com/2004/04/06/business/many-hospitals-resist-computerized-patient-care.html?scp=1&sq=cedar%20sinai%20electronic%20health%20record&st=cse.

Han, Y.Y., J.A. Carcillo, S.T. Venkataraman, R.S.B. Clark, R.S. Watson, T.C. Nguyen, H. Bayir, and R.A. Orr. 2005. Unexpected increased mortality after implementation of a commercially sold computerized physician order entry system. *Pediatrics* 116:1506-1512. http://pediatrics.aappublications.org/cgi/eletters/116/6/1506#1632.

Hann's On Software. 2008. Hann's On Software HL7 Interface Specification. Documentation Version: 4-1-2008. http://www.hosinc.com/Products/Interfaces/interface_documentation.htm#Give%20code/drug%20ID.

Harrison, M.I., R. Koppel, S. Bar-Lev. 2007. Unintended consequences of information technologies in health care—an interactive sociotechnical analysis. *Journal of the American Medical Informatics Association* 14(5):542-549.

Glaser, J. 2005 (June 13). Success factors for clinical information system implementation. *Hospital and Health Networks' Most Wired Magazine.* http://www.usafp.org/CHCSII-Files/Implementation-Files/Success%20Factors%20for%20Clinical%20Information%20System%20Implementation.pdf.

Appendix B

Kaplan, B. 1987. The Medical Computing 'Lag': Perceptions of Barriers to the Application of Computers to Medicine. *International Journal of Technology Assessment in Health Care* 3(1):123-136.

Kaplan, B. 2001a. Evaluating informatics applications—Review of the clinical decision support systems evaluation literature. *International Journal of Medical Informatics* 64(1):15-37.

Kaplan, B. 2001b. Evaluating informatics applications—Social interactionism and call for methodological pluralism. *International Journal of Medical Informatics* 64(1):39-56.

Kaplan, B. and K.J. Harris-Salamone. 2009. Health IT project success and failure: Recommendations from literature and an AMIA workshop. *Journal of the American Medical Informatics Association* 16(3):291-299.

Kaplan, B. and N. Shaw. 2004. Future directions in evaluation research: People, organizational, and social issues. *Methods of Information in Medicine* 43(3-4):215-231.

Kling, R., H. Crawford, H. Rosenbaum, S. Sawyer, S. Weisband. 2000 (August 14). Learning from social informatics: information and communication technologies in human contexts. Center for Social Informatics, Indiana University. http://rkcsi.indiana.edu/archive/SI/Arts/SI_report_Aug_14.doc.

Kling R., H. Rosenbaum, and S. Sawyer. 2005. *Understanding and Communicating Social Informatics: A Framework for Studying and Teaching the Human Contexts of Information and Communication Technologies.* Medford, NJ: Information Today Press. 107-108.

Kling, R. and S. Iaconno. 1988. The mobilization of support for computerization: The role of computerization movements. *Social Problems* 34:226-243.

Koppel, R., J.P. Metlay, A. Cohen, B. Abaluck, A.R. Localio, S.E. Kimmel, B.L. Strom. 2005. Role of computerized physician order entry systems in facilitating medication errors. *Journal of the American Medical Association* 293:1197-1203. http://jama.ama-assn.org/cgi/content/abstract/293/10/1197.

Lorenzi, N.M., L.L. Novak, J.B. Weiss, C.S. Gadd, and K.M. Unertl. 2008. Crossing the implementation chasm: A proposal for bold action. *Journal of the American Medical Informatics Association*. 15(3):290-296.

Markus, M.L. and R.I. Benjamin.1997. The magic bullet theory in IT-enabled transformation. *Sloan Management Review* 38(2):55-68.

Obama, B. Address to Joint Session of the Congress, February 24, 2009. Public Papers of the Presidents of the United States. Washington, D.C.: Government Printing Office, 2004. http://www.gpo.gov/fdsys/pkg/DCPD-200900105/pdf/DCPD-200900105.pdf.

Office of Government Commerce. 2009. PRINCE2. http://www.ogc.gov.uk/methods_prince_2.asp.

Peel, L. and D. Rose. 2009 (Jan. 27). MPs point to 'further delays and turmoil' for £12.4 billion NHS computer upgrade. Times Online. http://www.timesonline.co.uk/tol/news/uk/article5596213.ece.

Pizzi, R. 2007 (Octover 30). EHR adoption an 'ugly process,' but CCHIT can improve appeal. *Healthcare IT News.* http://www.healthcareitnews.com/news/ehr-adoption-ugly-process-cchit-can-improve-appeal.

Rogers, E.M. 2003. *Diffusion of Innovations*, 5th ed. New York: The Free Press.

RTI Health, Social, and Economics Research. 2002. *The Economic Impacts of Inadequate Infrastructure for Software Testing Final Report.* National Institute of Standards and Technology. http://www.nist.gov/director/prog-ofc/report02-3.pdf.

Silverstein, S. 2006. Access patterns to a website on healthcare IT failure. AMIA 2006 Annual Meeting, poster session. http://www.ischool.drexel.edu/faculty/ssilverstein/AMIA_poster_Nov_2006.ppt.

Simon, S.R. C.S. Soran, R. Kaushal, C.A. Jenter, L.A. Volk, E. Burdick, P.D. Cleary, E.J. Orav, E.G. Poon, and D.W. Bates. 2009. Physicians' usage of key functions in electronic health records from 2005 to 2007: A statewide survey. *Journal of the American Medical Informatics Association* 16(4):465-470.

Star, S.L. and K. Ruhleder. 1996. Steps towards an ecology of infrastructure: Design and access for large information spaces. *Information Systems Research* (7):111-135.

Zhou, Li, C.S. Soran, C.A. Jenter, L.A. Volk, E.J. Orav, D.W. Bates, and S.R. Simon. 2009. The relationship between electronic health record use and quality of care over time. *Journal of the American Medical Informatics Association* 16(4):457-464.

Additional Resources

General

The Standish Group. 1995. *Chaos Report.* http://net.educause.edu/ir/library/pdf/NCP08083B.pdf.

The Standish Group. 2001. Extreme CHAOS. http://www.quarrygroup.com/wp-content/uploads/art-standishgrou-CHAOS0report.pdf.

Healthcare

Success and Failure Factors - Research Papers

Brender, J., E. Ammenwerth, P. Nykänen, and J. Talmon. 2006. Factors influencing success and failure of health informatics systems: A pilot Delphi study. *Methods of Information in Medicine* 45(1):125-136.

Heeks, R. 2006. Health information systems: Failure, success and improvisation. *International Journal of Medical Informatics* 75:125-137.

Kaplan, B. and K.D. Harris-Salamone. 2009. Health IT project success and failure: Recommendations from an AMIA workshop. *Journal American Medical Informatics Association* 16(3):291-299.

Ong, K. 2007. Why do projects fail? Chapter 16 in *Medical Informatics: An Executive Primer*. Edited by Ong, K. Chicago: HIMSS.

Paré, G., C. Sicotte, M. Jaana, and D. Girouard. 2008. Prioritizing the risk factors influencing the success of clinical information systems. *Methods of Information in Medicine* 47(3):251-259.

van der Meijden, M.J., H.H. Tange, J. Troost, and A. Hasman. 2003. Determinants of success of inpatient clinical information systems: A literature review. *Journal of the American Medical Informatics Association* 10(3):235-243.

Success and Failure Factors - Practitioner Advice

Glaser, J. 2004 (October). Management's role in IT project failure. *Healthcare Financial Management*. http://findarticles.com/p/articles/mi_m3257/is_10_58/ai_n6274067/.

Glaser, J. 2005 (January). More on management's role in IT project failure. *Healthcare Financial Management*. http://findarticles.com/p/articles/mi_m3257/is_1_59/ai_n8706921/.

Examples

Research Case Studies and Analyses

Aarts, J. and M. Berg. 2006. Same system, different outcomes. *Methods of Information in Medicine* 45:53-61.

Aarts, J., H. Doorewaard, and M. Berg. 2004. Understanding implementation: The case of a computerized physician order entry systems in a large Dutch university medical center. *Journal of the American Medical Informatics Association* 11(3):207-216.

Beynon-Davies, P. 1995. Information systems 'failure': The case of the London ambulance service computer-aided despatch project. *European Journal of Information Systems* 4:171-184.

Beynon-Davies, P. and M. Lloyd-Williams. 1999. When health information systems fail. *Topics in Health Information Management* 19(4):66-79.

Brown, A.D. and M.R. Jones. 1998. Doomed to failure: Narratives of inevitability and conspiracy in a failed IS project. *Organization Studies* 19(1):73-88.

Dowling, A.F. 1980. Do hospital staff interfere with computer system implementation? *Health Care Management Review* 5:23-32.

House of Commons Public Accounts Committee. 2009 (January 27). *The National Programme for IT in the NHS: Progress since 2006*. London: The Stationery Office Ltd. http://www.publications.parliament.uk/pa/cm200809/cmselect/cmpubacc/153/15302.htm.

Lundsgaarde, H.P., P.J. Fischer, and D.J. Steele. 1981. *Human Problems in Computerized Medicine*. Lawrence, KS: The University of Kansas.

Massaro, T.A. 1993. Introducing physician order entry at a major academic medical center. 1: Impact on organizational culture and behavior. *Academic Medicine* 68(1):20-25.

Massaro, T.A. 1993. Introducing physician order entry at a major academic medical center. 2: Impact on medical education. *Academic Medicine* 68(1):25-30.

Sicotte, C., J.L. Denis, and P. Lehoux. 1998. The computer-based patient record: A strategic issue in process innovation. *Journal of Medical Systems* 22(6):431-443.

Sicotte, C., J.L. Denis, P. Lehoux, and F. Champagne. 1998. The computer-based patient record: Challenges towards timeless and spaceless medical practice. *Journal of Medical Systems* 22(4):237-256.

Southon, F.G.C., C. Sauer, and C.N.G. Dampney. 1997. Information technology in complex health services: Organizational impediments to successful technology transfer and diffusion. *Journal of the American Medical Informatics Association* 4:112-124.

van't Riet, A., M. Berg, F. Hiddema, and S. Kees. 2001. Meeting patients' needs with patient information systems: Potential benefits from qualitative research methods. *International Journal of Medical Informatics* 64:1-14.

Wells, S. and C. Bullen. 2008. A near miss: The importance of context in a public health informatics project in a New Zealand case study. *Journal of the American Medical Informatics Association* 15(5):701-704.

Useful Compilations

European Federation of Medical Informatics. 2009. Bad health informatics can kill. http://iig.umit.at/efmi/badinformatics.htm.

Silverstein, S. 2007. Sociotechnologic issues in clinical computing: Common examples of healthcare IT difficulties. http://www.ischool.drexel.edu/faculty/ssilverstein/failurecases/?loc=home.

Unintended Consequences

Ash, J., M. Berg, and E.W. Coiera. 2004. Some unintended consequences of information technology in health care: The nature of patient care information system-related errors. *Journal of the American Medical Informatics Association* 11(2):104-112.

Campbell, E, D. Sittig, J. Ash, K. Guappone, and R. Dykstra. 2006. Types of unintended consequences related to computerized provider order entry. *Journal of the American Medical Informatics Association* 13(5):547-56.

Harrison, M.I., R. Koppel, and S. Bar-Lev. 2007. Unintended consequences of information technologies in health care: An interactive sociotechnical analysis. *Journal of the American Medical Informatics Association* 14(5):542-549.

Appendix B

Errors

Han, Y.Y., J.A. Carcillo, S.T. Venkataraman, R.S. Clark, R.S. Watson, T.C. Mguyen, H. Bayir, and R.A. Orr. 2005. Unexpected increased mortality after implementation of a commercially sold computerized physician order entry system. *Pediatrics* 116(6):1506-1512.

Koppel, R., J.P. Metlay, A. Cohen, B. Abaluck, A.R. Localio, S.E. Kimmel, and B. L. Strom. 2005. Role of computerized physician order entry systems in facilitating medication errors. *Journal of the American Medical Association* 293(10):1197-1203.

Sustainability

Wetter, T. 2007. To decay is system: The challenges of keeping a health information system alive. *International Journal of Medical Informatics* 76S:S252-S260.

Workarounds

Koppel, R., T. Wetterneck, J.L. Telles, and B-T. Karsh. 2008. Workarounds to barcode medication administration systems: Their occurrences, causes, and threats to patient safety. *Journal of the American Medical Informatics Association* 15(4):408-423.

Vogelsmeier, A.A., J.R.B. Halbersleben, and J.R. Scott-Cawiezell. 2008. Technology implementation and workarounds in the nursing home. *Journal of the American Medical Informatics Association* 15(1):114-119.

Appendix C

Analyzing Workflow for a Health IT Implementation

An Often Short-shrifted Step Is Essential in Successful IT Deployments

by Lydia Washington, MS, RHIA, CPHIMS

The inability to integrate electronic health records (EHRs) into clinician workflow is a well-documented barrier to implementing EHR systems. To address this problem, organizations must analyze their workflow processes before implementing an EHR system.

HIM professionals are well positioned to perform workflow analysis because they can see how individuals and organizational units work together. They also understand the flow and uses of information in their organization. A 2005 AHIMA study found that successful EHR system implementations are closely correlated with HIM participation in workflow analysis and process improvement in the clinical care setting and the HIM department.

Getting to Optimal

Optimal workflow requires having the right information at the right time so that the individual performing a step or task can advance the process toward completion. To achieve optimal workflow, organizations must take a step back and analyze the flow of work.

Workflow analysis, also known as process analysis, involves identifying, prioritizing, and ordering the tasks and information needed to achieve the intended result of a clinical or business process. Workflow analysis and process redesign are frequently omitted or overlooked when identifying and selecting new information technology. However, they are absolutely critical because of the inherent complexity in most healthcare clinical and administrative processes.

People and processes are core considerations that often do not receive the attention they need in order to make an IT project successful. It is an old truism that even the worst technology can be made to work in an environment where people understand and are committed to making it work, while a technologically superior product can languish on a shelf because environmental factors, such as people and process issues, prohibit it from being successful. Workflow analysis mitigates these risks and increases the chances for success in an IT implementation.

Techniques and Tools

Workflow analysis involves applying a set of techniques that identify and address environmental factors and information needs in the early stages of system selection and implementation. These techniques are used to:

- Identify the boundaries of a process
- Establish a common understanding of its triggers, steps, and results among stakeholders
- Analyze how the current process functions
- Understand where it can be streamlined and otherwise improved
- Develop use cases that will guide the design, development, and support of the new system that automates the process

The methods employed to understand current and future state processes usually include brainstorming with process stakeholders, simple observation, and the use of tools such as checklists and activity logs. Information about the process is captured through a wide variety of tools such as process flow charts, workflow movement diagrams, swim lane charts, and fish bone diagrams.

Workflow documentation methods may range from those as simple as arranging sticky notes on a wall or drawing on a flipchart to capturing all nuances of a process with sophisticated software that facilitates continual refinement of the information within the team.

Equally as important as documenting current process is understanding the enablers or environmental factors that collectively determine how well or how poorly the process works.

Process Enablers

Key process enablers include:

- Policies and procedures that reflect the values and biases of the organization. These are part of and reflect the organizational culture in which work must be performed.
- Facilities or the physical environment that affect how tasks are accomplished, including factors such as amount and location of space, seating, work surfaces, lighting, equipment, and storage.
- Human resources, including the work force's current skill sets, workload, and the performance standards to which staff are expected to adhere.
- Motivation and commitment—the dynamics of what motivates the actors in the process to perform in a certain way and how they are rewarded or punished. This is arguably the single most important process enabler. Lack of motivation and commitment more than any other single factor affects the degree of success of a work process.
- Workflow design—rework, redundancies, bottlenecks, data loss, and other things that contribute to a poor process and create potential for errors, delays, additional cost, and safety and quality of care issues.
- Information technology and its usability—unintelligible error messages, confusing screen layouts, navigational dead ends, and lack of tech support are examples of how IT can adversely affect work processes.

All process enablers must be considered individually for solid process redesign. In addition, in healthcare, there are often unseen parts of a process that involve application of clinical knowledge. Failing to consider the unseen parts of a process can pose significant risks to obtaining a thorough and complete understanding of how a clinical process needs to work.

Clinical IT users are really knowledge workers, and their work frequently involves integrating knowledge and information from a variety of sources, including their own personal experiences. This must be factored into clinical process workflow.

Data Capture

If a key goal of workflow analysis is the design of new and improved processes that optimize workflow by delivering the right information at the appropriate point, then data capture is a prime consideration. As an integral part of workflow, data capture is the point of human-computer interface, and as such it provides the greatest opportunity to improve clinical and business processes. It also presents the greatest risk of the system and process not working as desired or the point of greatest user dissatisfaction.

Capture of health information usually includes inputs such as dictation and speech processing, use of templates, imaging of handwritten documents, and keyboard or point-and-click data entry. The choice of data capture technology affects how information will be structured—as discrete data or as unstructured text—and how the captured information can be used in the future. Workflow analysis will help determine whether structured or unstructured data are most appropriate for a given scenario.

For example, entry of structured data into a documentation template may be appropriate for a routine wellness exam in a clinic, but it may be insufficient to document a complex treatment or procedure with complications where it would be easier and faster for the clinician to dictate. Each process should be carefully evaluated to determine the most preferable methods. It is usually necessary to provide a range of data capture options that accommodate multiple preferences, purposes, and needs.

No Perfect System

The introduction of any new technology makes it impossible to continue doing business as usual. There are no perfect information systems, and in order to realize optimal benefit and minimize disruptions to the care and business processes, it is essential to conduct workflow analysis and process redesign. Obtaining a thorough understanding of business and clinical processes, their drivers and desired outcomes, is absolutely essential in the successful implementation of health IT.

References

Fenton, Susan, Margret Amatayakul, and Mitch Work. "The HIM Impact on EHRs." *Journal of AHIMA* 77, no. 9 (Oct. 2006): 36–40.

Mueller, M.L., et al. "Workflow Analysis and Evidence-based Medicine: Towards Integration of Knowledge-based Functions in Hospital Information Systems." *Proceedings/AMIA Annual Symposium* (1999): 330–34.

Sharp, Alec, and Patrick McDermott. *Workflow Modeling: Tools for Process Improvement and Application Development.* Norwoord, MA: Artech House, 2001.

Trachtenbarg, David E. "EHRs Fix Everything and Nine Other Myths." *Family Practice Management,* March 2007. Available online at www.aafp.org/fpm/20070300/26ehrs.html.

Lydia Washington (lydia.washington@ahima.org) is a practice manager at AHIMA.

Article citation:

Washington, Lydia. "Analyzing Workflow for a Health IT Implementation." *Journal of AHIMA* 79, no.1 (January 2008): 64-65.

Appendix D

Essential People Skills for EHR Implementation Success

For most HIM professionals (as well as nurses, physicians, and IT staff) a successful electronic health record (EHR) implementation is a top priority. AHIMA has provided support for this effort with its various e-HIM â work groups and will continue to do so.[1,2] The majority of these efforts have focused on EHR technology and ensuring that new technology meets the basic requirements of a legal and complete health record. Adequate technology and an understanding of that technology are necessary, but they are not enough for a successful EHR implementation. There have been plenty of well-funded, large-scale implementations that have failed.[3]

Researchers and others involved in EHR implementations have found that people skills such as leadership, communication, and training are absolutely essential. Take for example a computerized physician order entry (CPOE) system. In a consensus statement outlining the considerations for a successful CPOE system, colleagues at a 2001 conference dealing with CPOE only listed technology once. Other considerations included motivation, vision, leadership, personnel, value, workflow, project management, training, support, and evaluation.[4]

In order to successfully implement an EHR system, organizations need effective change management and delineation in the various roles. Nancy Lorenzi, PhD, and Robert Riley, PhD, define change management as "the process by which an organization gets to its future state, its vision."[5] They also outline reasons for contemporary system failures, which include communication, culture, organizational issues, training, and leadership. In an introduction to the issue of change management, Lorenzi identified "managing change among people, process, and information technology so that the use of information is optimized" as a cornerstone for "developing a new information management paradigm for health care."[6]

This practice brief examines some of the literature on the success factors for EHR adoption and offers the essential people skills for all professionals involved in an EHR implementation. Tools that can assist in assessing individual and organizational readiness for change are also identified and discussed briefly.

Leadership

Although details of a successful EHR implementation may differ between case studies and journal articles, they all agree that leadership is important. Stephen Badger states, "If the senior team is united in its commitment to a project's success, that project will almost certainly succeed. If they are divided, then the project will often fail."[7] M.J. van der Meijden and colleagues find that management support and lines of authority must be clearly defined.[8] These conclusions are consistent with works by Joan Ash, Lorenzi, and a report from the American College of Medical Informatics, which all discuss the unwavering commitment of top-level leadership, a shared vision, and ownership of the project as vital to success.[9-11]

One frequently mentioned consideration leaders must make when implementing an EHR is cost. But costs may not be only monetary. Organizations may experience productivity losses and workflow disruptions during implementation.[12] Learning how to use a new technology takes time, and work may slow down. Employees may even refuse to use a system.[13] If senior leaders do not fully understand the costs associated with EHR implementation, they may begin to conclude the project is unsuccessful if productivity drops or employees and processes are unsettled during implementation. In reality, these are natural and expected occurrences.

One report states that "to be successful, health informatics systems need to support—or at least not be in conflict with—the organizational structures of the organization in which the systems are implemented."[14] When the organizational structures and workflows of the system are not taken into account, the results can be devastating, as in the case of a pediatric hospital that experienced increased mortality for a subset of critically ill patients after implementing CPOE (a crucial part of any EHR).[15]

In this study, the workflow of the unit accepting the critically ill children was altered and hospital policies were revised to meet the needs of the software. Although redesigning workflows is often necessary for an EHR implementation, leaders must establish patient care and patient safety as priorities and insist the technology support it.

Almost every piece of the literature mentions one key player for successful EHR implementation teams: the physician champion. This champion must be respected by his or her peers and must be able to communicate the leadership vision of an EHR.[16] Physicians often need to hear from other physicians how this new technology can help them deliver better patient care.

Without a committed leadership in place, EHR implementation is likely to fail. However, leaders cannot do it all. Leaders must consider the issues faced by the individual users.

Individual Users

Mark Twain once said, "It's not the progress I mind, it's the change I don't like." Change is often the crux of the matter. When implementing an entirely new technology or procedure, people must learn a new skill; however, they don't have to "unlearn," or change, an old skill. The EHR is not just an efficiency enhancement tool, it is also a transformational tool that will change how healthcare is delivered and how everyone, including consumers, think about healthcare.[17]

Research has demonstrated that most people do not necessarily resist change automatically but resist having change imposed upon them.[18] Thus, it is imperative that all types of stakeholders interacting with or affected by the EHR implementation be involved in the implementation planning and execution. More than one implementation has failed because physicians or other important groups were not included in the planning.[19]

EHR implementations are more successful if:

- People skills have the highest priority during all stages of the project. Employees and clinicians must be kept informed and engaged with planning and communication.[20]
- An attempt is made to determine what will motivate people to transition from paper to an EHR.[21]
- Users are involved in any analysis and redesign of their workflow.

- Users participate in the development and specification of the customizable portions of the EHR.
- Training (online, classes, one-on-one) is offered both pre- and post-implementation.[22]
- Extensive, intensive 24/7 support is included at and immediately following go-live.

Anna Marie Hostgaard and Christian Nohr showed that employee resistance to change is related to the way they experience the following conditions:

- Pressure about developing new skills
- Fear of looking stupid or incompetent in these new skill sets
- Fear of losing professional status
- Pressure connected with management expectations for improved performance and effectiveness
- Pressure connected with a perception of more control by management resulting in an expectation of fewer errors
- Fear of job loss due to the new technology[23]

Users at all levels of the organization need to feel that they are a part of the process and have at least a modicum of control over what is happening with their jobs. As Robert Braude noted, "acceptance of an information system by its intended users is the final stage in successful information systems implementation."[24]

Sample Tactics and Processes for Implementing Change

Tactics and Processes	Positive Impacts
Communication and involvement	More involved staff Better understanding of how the changes will impact the organization Better knowledge of the changes Better ability to cope with the changes
Design process • Process reengineering • Quality management efforts • Responsibility modeling • Site visits • Vendor demonstrations	Better systems design More effective work processes
Change management • Design of the change structure and process	Less stressful organizational change Smoother implementation Better acceptance of the changes Better management of the altered organization
Project management	Better implementation of systems
Training • Demonstrations • One-on-one • Classes • Discipline-specific examples	Better use of the new system Better management of the altered organization
Evaluation • Surveys • Interviews • Observations	Determination of actual vs. expected system outcomes Input data for process improvements in future implementation

Lorenzi, Nancy M., et al. "Antecedents of the People and Organizational Aspects of Medical Informatics: A Literature Review." *Journal of the American Medical Informatics Association* 4, no. 2 (1997): 79-93.

These are some of the benefits organizations can expect when they emphasize people, as well as technology, during an EHR implementation.

Communication

At the root of all people skills is communication at every level, whether it's from leadership to the organization about the vision, mission, plans, and support for the EHR implementation; between the project manager and leadership ensuring that leadership is aware of the status of the project and is not caught by surprise when problems arise; or between trainers and users regarding how the EHR fits into the users' work.

Richard Dykstra found that the implementation of CPOE had an impact on communication and that communication had an impact on the implementation of CPOE. Specific negative impacts were found in the following areas:

- The illusion of complete dependability—users have an unwarranted reliance on the computer system.
- A substitute for interpersonal communication. Person-to-person interaction builds team camaraderie. People now separate to work on the computer.
- Increased volume of communication due to rework.[25]

The physician-nurse relationship can also be affected negatively. Effective communication can require learning new methods and making a special effort. This effect was also reported in the Yong Han article reporting increased mortality.[26]

The research did not describe strong negative or positive impacts on communication between the medical care team and the patient. However, the nature of the communication was different. Some medical teams even found that CPOE increased their efficiency and productivity.[27] Over time, as people become familiar with CPOE and rearrange their workflow in a manner consistent with it, many of these problems will be forgotten. The important thing to keep in mind is that these and other communication problems are likely to occur during EHR implementation.

Training

Part of the communication plan is training. Ongoing training should be a part of an organization's EHR maintenance plan. Adequate training, from basic to advanced, is essential for EHR implementation success. Training should start from the time the plan is conceived. It should be ongoing because changes will be made to the software, employees will change jobs, and new employees will join the organization.

Organizations can incorporate a variety of strategies for training. AHIMA e-HIM practice briefs describe communication methods including letters, posters, videos, Intranet sites or pages, brown-bag sessions, demonstrations in physician and clinical lounges, fliers, and e-mail.[28,29] Other methods to consider are group sessions in a technology lab and even one-on-one with particularly recalcitrant users.

Tools

When preparing for an EHR implementation, it may be helpful to evaluate an organization's readiness for change and its acceptance of that change, both in its clinical and business units. Lorenzi and her colleagues have developed a success factor profile to assess units for implementation of a clinical computing innovation. In addition to the usual factors such as level of activity and technology infrastructure, they evaluated what they called "peopleware" and innovation prospects. Peopleware includes the staff experience with technology, previous responses to change, and current and potential technology change champions, among other factors. Innovation prospects included a department's desire to be a pilot site, its interpretation of the largest benefits and drawbacks, its technology wish list, and resources it could bring to the change.[30] When dealing with a complex implementation in a complex environment, there are few guarantees. However, simply evaluating for these criteria is likely to sensitize everyone, including the potential end users, to their importance.

Finally, when implementing the EHR it is important to get feedback from the end users to determine their acceptance and use of the system, as well as find out what they are looking for in the future. Reed Gardner and Henry Lundsgaarde performed this type of an evaluation using question categories that included user computer experience, attitudes about the impact of the system upon practice, opinions about the functionality, and desired future functionality.[31] Their article includes a list of the questions used in their research—a handy resource for building an evaluation.

Conclusion

Technology is necessary, but not sufficient, for a successful EHR implementation. This has been shown repeatedly. Lorenzi and Riley outline a number of reasons why people skills are important to EHR implementations, all with essentially the same message: dealing with complex human beings can be much more difficult than dealing with the new technology. However, the rewards can be well worth it, as the selection of positive impacts in the table at left illustrates. All HIM professionals are encouraged to make people issues a priority when implementing the EHR and its components.

Notes

1. AHIMA HIM Practice Transformation Work Group. "A Checklist for Assessing HIM Department Readiness and Planning for the EHR." *Journal of AHIMA* 76, no. 6 (2005): 56E-H.

2. AHIMA Work Group on Electronic Health Records Management. "The Strategic Importance of Electronic Health Records Management: Checklist for Transition to the EHR." *Journal of AHIMA* 75, no. 9 (2004): 80C-E.

3. Lorenzi, Nancy M., et al. "Antecedents of the People and Organizational Aspects of Medical Informatics: A Literature Review." *Journal of the American Medical Informatics Association* 4, no. 2 (1997): 79-93.

4. Ash, Joan S., Zoe Stavri, and Gilad J. Kuperman. "A Consensus Statement on Considerations for a Successful CPOE Implementation." *Journal of the American Medical Informatics Association* 10, no. 3 (2003): 229-34.

5. Lorenzi, Nancy M., and Robert T. Riley. "Managing Change: An Overview." *Journal of the American Medical Informatics Association* 7, no. 2 (2000): 116-24.

6. Lorenzi, Nancy M. "The Cornerstones of Medical Informatics." *Journal of the American Medical Informatics Association* 7, no. 2 (2000): 204.

7. Badger, Stephen L., Ryan G. Bosch, and Praveen Toteja. "CEO Leadership: Seven Strategies for Leading Successful EHR Implementations." Paper presentation. HIMSS 2006 Annual Conference and Exhibit, San Diego, CA.

8. van der Meijden, M.J., et al. "Determinants of Success of Inpatient Clinical Information Systems: A Literature Review." *Journal of the American Medical Informatics Association* 10, no. 3 (2003): 235-43.

9. Ash, Joan S., Zoe Stavri, and Gilad J. Kuperman. "A Consensus Statement on Considerations for a Successful CPOE Implementation." *Journal of the American Medical Informatics Association* 10, no. 3 (2003): 229-34.

10. Lorenzi, Nancy M., and Robert T. Riley. "Managing Change: An Overview."

11. Ash, Joan S., and David W. Bates. "Factors and Forces Affecting EHR System Adoption: Report of a 2004 ACMI Discussion." *Journal of the American Medical Informatics Association* 12, no. 1 (2005): 8-12.

12. Baron, Richard J., et al. "Electronic Health Records: Just around the Corner? Or over the Cliff?" *Annals of Internal Medicine* 143, no. 3 (2005): 222-26.

13. Ash, Joan S., and David W. Bates. "Factors and Forces Affecting EHR System Adoption: Report of a 2004 ACMI Discussion."

14. Doctor's Office Quality-Information Technology. "Electronic Health Record Implementation in Physician Offices: Critical Success Factors." 2005. Available online at www.delmarvafoundation.org/DOQ-IT/docs/EHR_Critical_Success_Factors.pdf.

15. Han, Yong Y., et al. "Unexpected Increased Mortality after Implementation of a Commercially Sold Computerized Physician Order Entry System." *Pediatrics* 116 (2005): 1506-12.

16. Ash, Joan S., Zoe Stavri, and Gilad J. Kuperman. "A Consensus Statement on Considerations for a Successful CPOE Implementation."

17. McLane, Sharon. "Designing an EMR Planning Process Based on Staff Attitudes toward and Opinions about Computers in Healthcare." *CIN: Computers, Informatics, Nursing* 23, no. 2 (2005): 85-92.

18. Lorenzi, Nancy M., and Robert T. Riley. "Managing Change: An Overview."

19. Scott, J. Tim, et al. "Kaiser Permanente's Experience of Implementing an Electronic Medical Record: A Qualitative Study." *British Medical Journal* 331 (2005): 13-16.

20. Ash, Joan S., Zoe Stavri, and Gilad J. Kuperman. "A Consensus Statement on Considerations for a Successful CPOE Implementation."

21. Ash, Joan S., and David W. Bates. "Factors and Forces Affecting EHR System Adoption: Report of a 2004 ACMI Discussion."

22. Ash, Joan S., Zoe Stavri, and Gilad J. Kuperman. "A Consensus Statement on Considerations for a Successful CPOE Implementation."

23. Hostgaard, Anna Marie, and Christian Nohr. "Dealing with Organizational Change when Implementing EHR Systems." Paper presentation. MEDINFO 2004, San Francisco, CA.

24. Braude, Robert. "People and Organizational Issues in Health Informatics." *Journal of the American Medical Informatics Association* 4, no. 2 (1997): 150-51.

25. Dykstra, Richard. "Computerized Physician Order Entry and Communication: Reciprocal Impacts." Paper presentation. 2002 AMIA Annual Symposium, San Antonio, TX.

26. Han, Yong Y., et al. "Unexpected Increased Mortality after Implementation of a Commercially Sold Computerized Physician Order Entry System."

27. Dykstra, Richard. "Computerized Physician Order Entry and Communication: Reciprocal Impacts."

28. AHIMA HIM Practice Transformation Work Group. "A Checklist for Assessing HIM Department Readiness and Planning for the EHR."

29. AHIMA Work Group on Electronic Health Records Management. "The Strategic Importance of Electronic Health Records Management: Checklist for Transition to the EHR."

30. Lorenzi, Nancy M., et al. "The Success Factor Profile for Clinical Computer Innovation." Paper presentation. MEDINFO 2004, San Francisco, CA.

31. Gardner, Reed M., and Henry P. Lundsgaarde. "Evaluation of User Acceptance of a Clinical Expert System." *Journal of the American Medical Informatics Association* 1, no. 6 (1994): 428-38.

Prepared by

Susan H. Fenton, MBA, RHIA, Kathy Giannangelo, RHIA, CCS, and Mary Stanfill, RHIA, CCS, CCS-P

Article citation

Fenton, Susan H., Giannangelo, Kathy, Stanfill, Mary. "Essential People Skills for EHR Implementation Success (AHIMA Practice Brief)." Journal of AHIMA 77, no.6 (June 2006): 60A-D.

Appendix E

Federal Agencies' Demonstrate Challenges to Successful Implementation

United States Government Accountability Office

Testimony
Before the Committee on Health,
Education, Labor, and Pensions
U.S. Senate

For Release on Delivery
Expected at 10:00 a.m. EST
January 15, 2009

HEALTH INFORMATION TECHNOLOGY

Federal Agencies' Experiences Demonstrate Challenges to Successful Implementation

Statement of Valerie C. Melvin, Director
Human Capital and Management Information Systems
Issues

GAO-09-312T

Highlights of GAO-09-312T, a hearing before the Senate Committee on Health, Education, Labor, and Pensions.

January 15, 2009

HEALTH INFORMATION TECHNOLOGY

Federal Agencies' Experiences Demonstrate Challenges to Successful Implementation

Why GAO Did This Study

As GAO and others have reported, the use of information technology (IT) has enormous potential to help improve the quality of health care and is important for improving the performance of the U.S. health care system. Given its role in providing health care, the federal government has been urged to take a leadership role to improve the quality and effectiveness of health care, and it has been working to promote the nationwide use of health IT for a number of years. However, achieving widespread adoption and implementation of health IT has proven challenging, and the best way to accomplish this transition remains subject to much debate.

At the committee's request, this testimony discusses important issues identified by GAO's work that have broad relevance to the successful implementation of health IT to improve the quality of health care.

To develop this testimony, GAO relied largely on its previous work on federal health IT activities.

What GAO Found

Health IT has the potential to help improve the efficiency and quality of health care, but achieving the transition to a nationwide health IT capability is an inherently complex endeavor. A successful transition will require, among other things, addressing the following issues:

- *Establishing a foundation of clearly defined health IT standards that are agreed upon by all important stakeholders.* Developing, coordinating, and agreeing on standards are crucial for allowing health IT systems to work together and to provide the right people access to the information they need: for example, technology standards must be agreed on (such as file types and interchange systems), and a host of content issues must also be addressed (one example is the need for consistent medical terminology). Although important steps have been taken, additional effort is needed to define, adopt, and implement such standards to promote data quality and consistency, system interoperability (that is, the ability of automated systems to share and use information), and information protection.

- *Defining comprehensive plans that are grounded in results-oriented milestones and measures.* Using interoperable health IT to improve the quality and efficiency of health care is a complex goal that involves a range of stakeholders, various technologies, and numerous activities taking place over an expanse of time, and it is important that these activities be guided by comprehensive plans that include milestones and performance measures. Without such plans, it will be difficult to ensure that the many activities are coordinated, their results monitored, and their outcomes most effectively integrated.

- *Implementing an approach to protection of personal privacy that encourages public acceptance of health IT.* A robust approach to privacy protection is essential to establish the high degree of public confidence and trust needed to encourage widespread adoption of health IT and particularly electronic medical records. Health IT programs and applications need to address key privacy principles (for example, the access principle, which establishes the right of individuals to review certain personal health information). At the same time, they need to overcome key challenges (for example, those related to variations in states' privacy laws). Unless these principles and challenges are fully and adequately addressed, there is reduced assurance that privacy protection measures will be consistently built into health IT programs and applications, and public acceptance of health IT may be put at risk.

To view the full product, including the scope and methodology, click on GAO-09-312T. For more information, contact Valerie Melvin at (202) 512-6304 or melvinv@gao.gov.

United States Government Accountability Office

Appendix E

Mr. Chairman and Members of the Committee:

I am pleased to be here today to comment on federal efforts to advance the use of health information technology (IT). Studies published by the Institute of Medicine and others have long indicated that fragmented, disorganized, and inaccessible clinical information adversely affects the quality of health care and compromises patient safety. Further, long-standing problems with medical errors and inefficiencies have contributed to increased costs of health care. With health care spending in 2007 reaching approximately $2.2 trillion, or 16 percent of the U.S. gross domestic product, concerns about the costs of health care have continued to grow, and have prompted calls from policy makers, industry experts, and medical practitioners to improve the U.S. health care system.

As has been recognized by you and other members of Congress, as well as President Bush and President-elect Obama, the use of information technology to electronically collect, store, retrieve, and transfer clinical, administrative, and financial health information has great potential to help improve the quality and efficiency of health care. The successful implementation of health IT offers promise for improving patient safety and reducing inefficiencies and has been shown to support cost savings and other benefits. At the same time, successfully achieving widespread adoption and implementation of health IT has proven challenging, and the best way to accomplish this goal remains subject to much debate. According to the Department of Health and Human Services (HHS), only a small number of U.S. health care providers have fully adopted health IT due to significant financial, technical, cultural, and legal barriers, such as a lack of access to capital, a lack of data standards, and resistance from health care providers.

Given its role in providing health care, the federal government has been urged to take a leadership role to improve the quality and effectiveness of health care and has been working to promote the nationwide use of health IT for a number of years. In April 2004, President Bush issued an executive order that called for widespread adoption of interoperable electronic health records by 2014,[1] and HHS, in turn, initiated activities to advance the nationwide implementation of interoperable health IT. In addition, for the past decade, the Departments of Defense (DOD) and Veterans Affairs (VA) have been pursuing initiatives to share data between their health information systems. In an effort to expedite the exchange of electronic health information between the two departments, the National Defense Authorization Act for Fiscal Year 2008[2] included provisions directing the two departments to jointly develop and implement, by September 30, 2009, fully interoperable[3] electronic health record systems or capabilities.

Since 2001, we have been reviewing aspects of the various federal efforts undertaken to implement information technology for health care and public health solutions. We have reported both on HHS's national health IT initiatives as well as on DOD's and VA's electronic health information sharing initiatives.[4] Overall, our studies have recognized progress made by these departments, but we have also pointed out areas of concern that could jeopardize their success in advancing the use of interoperable health IT. At your request, my testimony today discusses important issues identified by our work

---

[1]Executive Order 13335, *Incentives for the Use of Health Information Technology and Establishing the Position of the National Health Information Technology Coordinator* (Washington, D.C.: Apr. 27, 2004).

[2]Pub. L. No. 110-181, § 1635 (2008).

[3]Interoperability is the ability of two or more systems or components to exchange information and to use the information that has been exchanged.

[4]GAO, *Computer-Based Patient Records: Better Planning and Oversight by VA, DOD, and IHS Would Enhance Health Data Sharing*, GAO-01-459 (Washington, D.C.: Apr. 30, 2001); *Computer-Based Patient Records: VA and DOD Efforts to Exchange Health Data Could Benefit from Improved Planning and Project Management*, GAO-04-687 (Washington, D.C.: June 7, 2004); *Health Information Technology: HHS Is Taking Steps to Develop a National Strategy*, GAO-05-628 (Washington, D.C.: May 27, 2005); *Health Information Technology: HHS Is Continuing Efforts to Define its National Strategy*, GAO-06-1071T (Washington, D.C.: Sept. 1, 2006); *Information Technology: DOD and VA Have Increased Their Sharing of Health Information, but More Work Remains*, GAO-08-954 (Washington, D.C.: July 28, 2008); *Health Information Technology: HHS Has Taken Important Steps to Address Privacy Principles and Challenges, Although More Work Remains*, GAO-08-1138 (Washington, D.C.: Sept. 17, 2008); and *Electronic Health Records: DOD and VA Have Increased Their Sharing of Health Information, but Further Actions Are Needed*, GAO-08-1158T (Washington, D.C.: Sept. 24, 2008).

that have broad relevance to the successful implementation of health IT to further improve the quality of health care.

In developing this testimony, we relied largely on our previous work. We conducted our work in support of this testimony between December 2008 and January 2009 in Washington, D.C. All work on which this testimony is based was performed in accordance with generally accepted government auditing standards. Those standards require that we plan and perform audits to obtain sufficient, appropriate evidence to provide a reasonable basis for our findings and conclusions based on our audit objectives. We believe that the evidence obtained provides a reasonable basis for our findings and conclusions based on our audit objectives.

In summary, transitioning to a nationwide health IT capability is an inherently complex endeavor. Achieving this transition and the potential efficiencies and quality improvements promised by widespread adoption of health IT will require consideration of many serious issues, including the need for a foundation of clearly defined health IT standards that are agreed upon by all important stakeholders, comprehensive planning grounded in results-oriented milestones and measures, and an approach to privacy protection that encourages acceptance and adoption of electronic health records.

- Developing, coordinating, and agreeing on standards are crucial for allowing health IT systems to work together and to provide the right people access to the information they need. Any level of interoperability depends on the use of agreed-upon standards to ensure that information can be shared and used. Developing and implementing health IT standards requires structures and ongoing mechanisms that include the participation of the relevant stakeholders, in both the public and private health care sectors who will be sharing information. Although important steps have been taken, additional effort is needed to define, adopt, and implement such standards to promote data quality and consistency, system interoperability, and information protection.

- Using interoperable health IT to improve the quality and efficiency of health care is a complex goal that involves a range of stakeholders, various technologies, and numerous activities taking place over an expanse of time; in view of this complexity, it is important that these activities be guided by comprehensive plans that include milestones and performance measures. Milestones and performance measures allow the results of the activities to be monitored and assessed, so that corrective action can be taken if needed. Without comprehensive plans, it will be difficult to ensure that the many activities are coordinated, their results monitored, and their outcomes integrated.

- An important consideration in health IT is an overall approach for protecting the privacy of personal electronic health information. The capacity of health information exchange organizations to store and manage a large amount of electronic health information increases the risk that a breach in security could expose the personal health information of numerous individuals. Addressing and mitigating this risk is essential to encourage public acceptance of the increased use of health IT and electronic medical records. We have identified[5] key privacy principles that health IT programs and applications need to address[6] and key challenges that they need to overcome.[7] Unless these principles and challenges are fully and adequately addressed, there is reduced assurance that privacy protection measures will be

---

[5]GAO, *Health Information Technology: Early Efforts Initiated but Comprehensive Privacy Approach Needed for National Strategy*, GAO-07-238 (Washington, D.C.: Jan. 10, 2007).

[6]We based these privacy principles on our evaluation of the HHS Privacy Rule promulgated under the Administrative Simplification provisions of the Health Insurance Portability and Accountability Act of 1996 (HIPAA), which define the circumstances under which an individual's health information may be used or disclosed. For example, the uses and disclosures principle provides, among other things, limits to the circumstances in which an individual's protected heath information may be used or disclosed by covered entities, and the access principle establishes individuals' rights to review and obtain a copy of their protected health information held in a designated record set. For more details, see GAO-07-238.

[7]We identified key challenges associated with protecting personal health information based on input from selected stakeholders in health information exchange organizations. These challenges are understanding and resolving legal and policy issues (for example, those related to variations in states' privacy laws); ensuring that only the minimum amount of information necessary is disclosed to only those entities authorized to receive the information; ensuring individuals' rights to request access and amendments to their own health information; and implementing adequate security measures for protecting health information. See GAO-07-238.

Appendix E

consistently built into health IT programs and applications, and public acceptance of health IT may be put at risk.

Background

Health care in the United States is a highly decentralized system, with stakeholders that include not only the entire population as consumers of health care, but also all levels of government, health care providers such as medical centers and community hospitals, patient advocates, health professionals, major employers, nonprofit health organizations, insurance companies, commercial technology providers, and others. In this environment, clinical and other health-related information is stored in a complex collection of paper files, information systems, and organizations, but much of it continues to be stored and shared on paper.

Successfully implementing health IT to replace paper and manual processes has been shown to support benefits in both cost savings and improved quality of care. For example, we reported to this committee in 2003[8] that a 1,951-bed teaching hospital stated that it had realized about $8.6 million in annual savings by replacing outpatient paper medical charts with electronic medical records. This hospital also reported saving more than $2.8 million annually by replacing its manual process for managing medical records with an electronic process to provide access to laboratory results and reports. Other technologies, such as bar coding of certain human drug and biological product labels, have also been shown to save money and reduce medical errors. Health care organizations reported that IT contributed other benefits, such as shorter hospital stays, faster communication of test results, improved management of chronic diseases, and improved accuracy in capturing charges associated with diagnostic and procedure codes.

There is also potential benefit from improving and expanding existing health IT systems. We have reported that some hospitals are

---

[8]GAO, *Information Technology: Benefits Realized for Selected Health Care Functions*, GAO-04-224 (Washington, D.C.: Oct. 31, 2003).

expanding their IT systems to support improvements in quality of care. In April 2007,[9] we released a study on the processes used by eight hospitals to collect and submit data on their quality of care to HHS's Centers for Medicare & Medicaid Services (CMS). Among the hospitals we visited, officials noted that having electronic records was an advantage for collecting the quality data because electronic records were more accessible and legible than paper records, and the electronic quality data could also be used for other purposes (such as reminders to physicians). Officials at each of the hospitals reported using the quality data to make specific changes in their internal procedures designed to improve care. However, hospital officials also reported several limitations in their existing IT systems that constrained the ability to support the collection of their quality data. For example, hospitals reported having a mix of paper and electronic systems, having data recorded only as unstructured narrative or other text, and having multiple systems within a single hospital that could not access each other's data. Although it was expected to take several years, all the hospitals in our study were working to expand the scope and functionality of their IT systems.

This example illustrates, among other things, that making health care information electronically available depends on interoperability—that is, the ability of two or more systems or components to exchange information and to use the information that has been exchanged. This capability is important because it allows patients' electronic health information to move with them from provider to provider, regardless of where the information originated. If electronic health records conform to interoperability standards, they can be created, managed, and consulted by authorized clinicians and staff across more than one health care organization, thus providing patients and their caregivers the necessary information required for optimal care. (Paper-based health records—if available—also provide necessary information, but unlike electronic health records, do not provide automated

---

[9]GAO, *Hospital Quality Data: HHS Should Specify Steps and Time Frame for Using Information Technology to Collect and Submit Data*, GAO-07-320 (Washington, D.C.: Apr. 25, 2007).

145

decision support capabilities, such as alerts about a particular patient's health, or other advantages of automation.)

Interoperability may be achieved at different levels (see fig. 1). For example, at the highest level, electronic data are computable (that is, in a format that a computer can understand and act on to, for example, provide alerts to clinicians on drug allergies). At a lower level, electronic data are structured and viewable, but not computable. The value of data at this level is that they are structured so that data of interest to users are easier to find. At still a lower level, electronic data are unstructured and viewable, but not computable. With unstructured electronic data, a user would have to find needed or relevant information by searching uncategorized data.

146

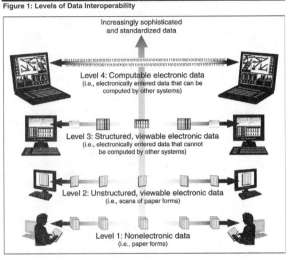

Figure 1: Levels of Data Interoperability

It is important to note that not all data require the same level of interoperability. For example, computable pharmacy and drug allergy data would allow automated alerts to help medical personnel avoid administering inappropriate drugs. On the other hand, for such narrative data as clinical notes, unstructured, viewable data may be sufficient. Achieving even a minimal level of electronic interoperability would potentially make relevant information available to clinicians.

Any level of interoperability depends on the use of agreed-upon standards to ensure that information can be shared and used. In the health IT field, standards may govern areas ranging from technical issues, such as file types and interchange systems, to content issues, such as medical terminology.

- For example, *vocabulary standards* provide common definitions and codes for medical terms and determine how information will be documented for diagnoses and procedures. These standards are intended to lead to consistent descriptions of a patient's medical condition by all practitioners. The use of common terminology helps in the clinical care delivery process, enables consistent data analysis from organization to organization, and facilitates transmission of information. Without such standards, the terms used to describe the same diagnoses and procedures may vary (the condition known as hepatitis, for example, may be described as a liver inflammation). The use of different terms to indicate the same condition or treatment complicates retrieval and reduces the reliability and consistency of data.

- Another example is *messaging standards*, which establish the order and sequence of data during transmission and provide for the uniform and predictable electronic exchange of data. These standards dictate the segments in a specific medical transmission. For example, they might require the first segment to include the patient's name, hospital number, and birth date. A series of subsequent segments might transmit the results of a complete blood count, dictating one result (e.g., iron content) per segment. Messaging standards can be adopted to enable intelligible communication between organizations via the Internet or some other communications pathway. Without them, the interoperability of health IT systems may be limited, reducing the data that can be shared.

Developing interoperability standards requires the participation of the relevant stakeholders who will be sharing information. In the case of health IT, stakeholders include both the public and private sectors. The public health system is made up of the federal, state, tribal, and local agencies that may deliver health care services to the population and monitor its health. Private health system participants include hospitals, physicians, pharmacies, nursing homes, and other organizations that deliver health care services to individual patients, as well as multiple vendors that provide health IT solutions.

GAO-09-312T

148

Federal Health IT Efforts Highlight Importance of Establishing Standards, Developing Comprehensive Plans, and Ensuring Privacy

Widespread adoption of health IT has the potential to improve the efficiency and quality of health care. However, transitioning to this capability is a challenging endeavor that requires attention to many important considerations. Among these are mechanisms to establish clearly defined health IT standards that are agreed upon by all important stakeholders, comprehensive planning grounded in results-oriented milestones and measures, and an approach to privacy protection that encourages acceptance and adoption of electronic health records. Attempting to expand the use of health IT without fully addressing these issues would put at risk the ultimate goal of achieving more effective health care.

Mechanisms and Structures for Harmonizing and Implementing Health IT Standards Are Essential to Enable Interoperability

The need for health care standards has been broadly recognized for a number of years. In previous work, we identified lessons learned by U.S. agencies and by other countries from their experiences. Among other lessons, they reported the need to define and adopt common standards and terminology to achieve data quality and consistency, system interoperability, and information protection.[10] In May 2003, we reported that federal agencies recognized the need for health care standards and were making efforts to strengthen and increase their use.[11] However, while they had made progress in defining standards, they had not met challenges in identifying and implementing standards necessary to support interoperability across the health care sector. We stated that until these challenges were addressed, agencies risked promulgating piecemeal and disparate systems unable to exchange data with each other when

---

[10]GAO, *Health Information Technology: HHS Is Taking Steps to Develop a National Strategy*, GAO-05-628 (Washington, D.C.: May 27, 2005).

[11]GAO, *Bioterrorism: Information Technology Strategy Could Strengthen Federal Agencies' Abilities to Respond to Public Health Emergencies*, GAO-03-139 (Washington, D.C.: May 30, 2003).

needed. We recommended that the Secretary of HHS define activities for ensuring that the various standards-setting organizations coordinate their efforts and reach further consensus on the definition and use of standards; establish milestones for defining and implementing standards; and create a mechanism to monitor the implementation of standards through the health care industry.

HHS implemented this recommendation through the activities of the Office of the National Coordinator for Health Information Technology (established within HHS in April 2004). Through the Office of the National Coordinator, HHS designated three primary organizations, made up of stakeholders from both the public and private health care sectors, to play major roles in identifying and implementing standards and expanding the implementation of health IT:

- The American Health Information Community (now known as the National eHealth Collaborative) was created by the Secretary of HHS to make recommendations on how to accelerate the development and adoption of health IT, including advancing interoperability, identifying health IT standards, advancing nationwide health information exchange, and protecting personal health information. Created in September 2005 as a federal advisory commission, the organization recently became a nonprofit membership organization. It includes representatives from both the public and private sectors, including high-level officials of VA and other federal and state agencies, as well as health systems, payers, health professionals, medical centers, community hospitals, patient advocates, major employers, nonprofit health organizations, commercial technology providers, and others. Among other things, the organization has identified health care areas of high priority and developed "use cases" for these areas (use cases are descriptions of events or scenarios, such as Public Health Case Reporting, that provide the context in which standards would be applicable, detailing what needs to be done to achieve a specific mission or goal).

- The Healthcare Information Technology Standards Panel (HITSP), sponsored by the American National Standards Institute[12] and funded by the Office of the National Coordinator, was established in October 2005 as a public-private partnership to identify competing standards for the use cases developed by the American Health Information Community and to "harmonize" the standards.[13] As of March 2008, nearly 400 organizations[14] representing consumers, healthcare providers, public health agencies, government agencies, standards developing organizations, and other stakeholders were participating in the panel and its committees. The panel also develops the interoperability specifications that are needed for implementing the standards. In collaboration with the National Institute for Standards and Technology, HITSP selected initial standards to address, among other things, requirements for message and document formats and for technical networking. Federal agencies that administer or sponsor federal health programs are now required to implement these standards, in accordance with an August 2006 Executive Order.[15]

- The Certification Commission for Healthcare Information Technology is an independent, nonprofit organization that certifies health IT products, such as electronic health records systems. HHS entered into a contract with the commission in October 2005 to

---

[12]The American National Standards Institute is a private, nonprofit organization whose mission is to promote and facilitate voluntary consensus standards and ensure their integrity.

[13]Harmonization is the process of identifying overlaps and gaps in relevant standards and developing recommendations to address these overlaps and gaps.

[14]Members include representatives from the following sectors: clinicians; providers; safety net providers and their representative organizations; vendors that develop, market, install, and support health IT products; healthcare purchasers or employers; healthcare payers or health insurance companies; public health professionals; national organizations with a broad representation of stakeholders with an interest in healthcare IT standards; clinical and health-services researchers' representative organizations; federal, state, and local agencies; coordinating bodies with responsibilities for and/or a relationship to healthcare IT used in the public sector; and consumer organizations with an interest in health IT standards.

[15]Executive Order 13410, *Promoting Quality and Efficient Health Care in Federal Government Administered or Sponsored Health Care Programs* (Washington, D.C.: Aug. 22, 2006).

develop and evaluate the certification criteria and inspection process for electronic health records. HHS describes certification as the process by which vendors' health IT systems are established to meet interoperability standards. The certification criteria defined by the commission incorporate the interoperability standards and specifications defined by HITSP. The results of this effort are intended to help encourage health care providers throughout the nation to implement electronic health records by giving them assurance that the systems will provide needed capabilities (including ensuring security and confidentiality) and that the electronic records will work with other systems without reprogramming.[16]

The interconnected work of these organizations to identify and promote the implementation of standards is important to the overall effort to advance the use of interoperable health IT. For example, according to HHS, the HITSP standards are incorporated into the National Coordinator's ongoing initiative to enable health care entities—such as providers, hospitals, and clinical labs—to exchange electronic health information on a nationwide basis. Under this initiative, HHS awarded contracts to nine regional and state health information exchanges as part of its efforts to provide prototypes of nationwide networks of health information exchanges.[17] Such exchanges are intended to eventually form a "network of networks" that is to produce the envisioned Nationwide Health Information Network (NHIN). According to HHS, the department planned to demonstrate the experiences and lessons learned from this work in December 2008, including defining specifications based upon the work of HITSP and standards development organizations to facilitate interoperable data exchange

---

[16]In May 2006, HHS finalized a process and criteria for certifying the interoperability of outpatient electronic health records and described criteria for future certification requirements. Certification criteria for inpatient electronic health records were finalized in June 2007. To date, the Certification Commission reports that it has certified about 140 products offering electronic health records.

[17]These exchanges are intended to connect providers and patients from different regions of the country and enable the sharing of electronic health information, such as health records and laboratory results. DOD, VA, and the Indian Health Service are participating in a federal component of this initiative.

among the participants, testing interoperability against these specifications, and developing trust agreements among participants to protect the information exchanged. HHS plans to place the nationwide health information exchange specifications defined by the participating organizations, as well as related testing materials, in the public domain, so that they can be used by other health information exchange organizations to guide their efforts to adopt interoperable health IT.

The products of the federal standards initiatives are also being used by DOD and VA in their ongoing efforts to achieve the seamless exchange of health information on military personnel and veterans. The two departments have committed to the goal of adopting applicable current and emerging HITSP standards. According to department officials, DOD is also taking steps to ensure compliance with standards through certification. To ensure that the electronic health records produced by the department's modernized health information system, AHLTA,[18] are compliant with standards, it is arranging for certification through the Certification Commission for Healthcare Information Technology. Both departments are also participating in the National Coordinator's standards initiatives. The involvement of the departments in these activities is an important mechanism for aligning their electronic health records with emerging federal standards.

Federal efforts to implement health IT standards are ongoing and some progress has been made. However, until agencies are able to demonstrate interoperable health information exchange between stakeholders on a broader level, the overall effectiveness of their efforts will remain unclear. In this regard, continued work on standards initiatives will remain essential for extending the use of health IT and fully achieving its potential benefits, particularly as both information technology and medicine advance.

---

[18]AHLTA originally was an acronym for Armed Forces Health Longitudinal Technology Application. The department no longer considers AHLTA an acronym but the official name of the system.

GAO-09-312T

153

Appendix E

Comprehensive Planning with Milestones and Performance Measures Is Essential to Achieving Health IT Goals

Using interoperable health IT to help improve the efficiency and quality of health care is a complex goal that involves a range of stakeholders and numerous activities taking place over an expanse of time; in view of this complexity, it is important to develop comprehensive plans that are grounded in results-oriented milestones and performance measures. Without comprehensive plans, it is difficult to coordinate the many activities under way and integrate their outcomes. Milestones and performance measures allow the results of the activities to be monitored and assessed, so that corrective action can be taken if needed.

Since it was established in 2004, the Office of the National Coordinator has pursued a number of health IT initiatives (some of which we described above), aimed at the expansion of electronic health records, identification of interoperability standards, advancement of nationwide health information exchange, and protection of personal health information.[19] It also developed a framework for strategic action for achieving an interoperable national infrastructure for health IT, which was released in 2004. We have noted accomplishments resulting from these various initiatives, but we also observed that the strategic framework did not include the detailed plans, milestones, and performance measures needed to ensure that the department integrated the outcomes of its various health IT initiatives and met its overall goals.[20] Given the many activities to be coordinated and the many stakeholders involved, we recommended in May 2005 that HHS define a national strategy for health IT that would include the necessary detailed plans, milestones, and performance measures, which are essential to help ensure progress toward the President's

---

[19]In prior work, we described programs that other divisions within HHS, such as the Agency for Healthcare Research and Quality and the Health Resources and Services Administration, administer to provide funding to organizations engaged in building and testing health IT systems, standards, and projects. See GAO-05-628 for a description of these activities.

[20]GAO, *Health Information Technology: HHS Is Taking Steps to Develop a National Strategy*, GAO-05-628 (Washington, D.C.: May 27, 2005).

goal for most Americans to have access to interoperable electronic health records by 2014. The department agreed with our recommendation, and in June 2008 it released a four-year strategic plan. If the plan's milestones and measures for achieving an interoperable nationwide infrastructure for health IT are appropriate and properly implemented, the plan could help ensure that HHS's various health IT initiatives are integrated and provide a useful roadmap to support the goal of widespread adoption of interoperable electronic health records.[21]

Across our health IT work at HHS and elsewhere, we have seen other instances in which planning activities have not been sufficiently comprehensive. An example is the experience of DOD and VA, which have faced considerable challenges in project planning and management in the course of their work on the seamless exchange of electronic health information. As far back as 2001 and 2002, we noted management weaknesses, such as inadequate accountability and poor planning and oversight, and recommended that the departments apply principles of sound project management.[22] The departments' efforts to meet the recent requirements of the National Defense Authorization Act for Fiscal Year 2008 provide additional examples of such challenges, raising concerns regarding their ability to meet the September 2009 deadline for developing and implementing interoperable electronic health record systems or capabilities. In July 2008, we identified steps that the departments had taken to establish an interagency program office and implementation plan, as required. According to the departments, they intended the program office to play a crucial role in accelerating efforts to achieve electronic health records and capabilities that allow for full interoperability, and they had

---

[21]In another example, as a result of the 2007 study of hospital quality data collection mentioned earlier, we recommended that the Secretary of HHS identify the specific steps that the department planned to take to promote the use of health IT for the collection and submission of these data, and that it inform interested parties of those steps and the expected time frame, including milestones for completing them.

[22]GAO, *Computer-Based Patient Records: Better Planning and Oversight by VA, DOD, and IHS Would Enhance Health Data Sharing*, GAO-01-459 (Washington, D.C.: Apr. 30, 2001) and *Veterans Affairs: Sustained Management Attention Is Key to Achieving Information Technology Results*, GAO-02-703 (Washington, D.C.: June 12, 2002).

GAO-09-312T

appointed an Acting Director from DOD and an Acting Deputy Director from VA. According to the Acting Director, the departments also have detailed staff and provided temporary space and equipment to a transition team. However, the newly established program office was not expected to be fully operational until the end of 2008—allowing the departments at most 9 months to meet the deadline for full interoperability.

Further, we reported other planning and management weaknesses. For example, the departments developed a DOD/VA Information Interoperability Plan in September 2008, which is intended to address interoperability issues and define tasks required to guide the development and implementation of an interoperable electronic health record capability. Although the plan included milestones and schedules, it was lacking many milestones for completing the activities defined in the plan. Accordingly, we recommended that the departments give priority to fully establishing the interagency program office and finalizing the implementation plan. Without an effective plan and a program office to ensure its implementation, the risk is increased that the two departments will not be able to meet the September 2009 deadline.

Establishing a Consistent Approach to Privacy Protection Is Essential for Encouraging Acceptance and Adoption of Health IT

As the use of electronic health information exchange increases, so does the need to protect personal health information from inappropriate disclosure. The capacity of health information exchange organizations to store and manage a large amount of electronic health information increases the risk that a breach in security could expose the personal health information of numerous individuals. Addressing and mitigating this risk is essential to encourage public acceptance of the increased use of health IT and electronic medical records.

Recognizing the importance of privacy protection, HHS included security and privacy measures in its 2004 framework for strategic action, and in September 2005, it awarded a contract to the Health Information Security and Privacy Collaboration as part of its efforts to provide a nationwide synthesis of information to inform privacy

GAO-09-312T

156

and security policymaking at federal, state, and local levels. The collaboration selected 33 states and Puerto Rico as locations in which to perform assessments of organization-level privacy- and security-related policies and practices that affect interoperable electronic health information exchange and their bases, including laws and regulations. As a result of this work, HHS developed and made available to the public a toolkit to guide health information exchange organizations in conducting assessments of business practices, policies, and state laws that govern the privacy and security of health information exchange.[23]

However, we reported in January 2007 that HHS initiated these and other important privacy-related efforts[24] without first defining an overall approach for protecting privacy. In our report, we identified key privacy principles and challenges to protecting electronic personal health information.

- Examples of principles that health IT programs and applications need to address include the uses and disclosures principle, which provides limits to the circumstances in which an individual's protected heath information may be used or disclosed, and the access principle, which establishes individuals' rights to review and obtain a copy of their protected health information in certain circumstances.[25]

---

[23]In June 2007, HHS reported the outcomes of its privacy and security solutions contract based on the work of 34 states and territories that participated in the contract. A final summary report described variations among organization-level business practices, policies, and laws for protecting health information that could affect organizations' abilities to exchange data.

[24]Our January 2007 report (GAO-07-238) describes various privacy-related efforts incorporated into HHS's overall health IT initiative, including the activities of the American Health Information Community, the Healthcare Information Technical Standards Panel, the Certification Commission for Healthcare IT, and the Nationwide Health Information Network.

[25]We based these privacy principles on our evaluation of the HHS Privacy Rule promulgated under the Administrative Simplification provisions of the Health Insurance Portability and Accountability Act of 1996 (HIPAA), which define the circumstances under which an individual's health information may be used or disclosed.

- Key challenges include understanding and resolving legal and policy issues (for example, those related to variations in states' privacy laws), ensuring that only the minimum amount of information necessary is disclosed to only those entities authorized to receive the information, ensuring individuals' rights to request access and amendments to their own health information, and implementing adequate security measures for protecting health information.[26]

We recommended that HHS define and implement an overall privacy approach that identifies milestones for integrating the outcomes of its privacy-related initiatives, ensures that key privacy principles are fully addressed, and addresses challenges associated with the nationwide exchange of health information.

In September 2008, we reported that HHS had begun to establish an overall approach for protecting the privacy of personal electronic health information—for example, it had identified milestones and an entity responsible for integrating the outcomes of its many privacy-related initiatives.[27] Further, the federal health IT strategic plan released in June 2008 includes privacy and security objectives along with strategies and target dates for achieving them.

However, in our view, more actions are needed. Specifically, within its approach, the department had not defined a process to ensure that the key privacy principles and challenges we had identified were fully and adequately addressed. This process should include, for example, steps for ensuring that all stakeholders' contributions to defining privacy-related activities are appropriately considered and that individual inputs to the privacy framework are effectively assessed and prioritized to achieve comprehensive coverage of all key privacy principles and challenges. Without such a process, stakeholders may lack the overall policies and guidance needed to assist them in their efforts to ensure that privacy protection

---

[26]We identified key challenges associated with protecting personal health information based on input from selected stakeholders in health information exchange organizations.

[27]GAO, *Health Information Technology: HHS Has Taken Important Steps to Address Privacy Principles and Challenges, Although More Work Remains*, GAO-08-1138 (Washington, D.C.: Sept. 17, 2008).

measures are consistently built into health IT programs and applications. Moreover, the department may miss an opportunity to establish the high degree of public confidence and trust needed to help ensure the success of a nationwide health information network. To address these concerns, we recommended in our September report that HHS include in its overall privacy approach a process for ensuring that key privacy principles and challenges are completely and adequately addressed.

Lacking an overall approach for protecting the privacy of personal electronic health information, there is reduced assurance that privacy protection measures will be consistently built into health IT programs and applications. Without such assurance, public acceptance of health IT may be at risk.

In closing, Mr. Chairman, many important steps have been taken, but more is needed before we can make a successful transition to a nationwide health IT capability and take full advantage of potential improvements in care and efficiency that this could enable. It is important to have structures and mechanisms to build, maintain, and expand a robust foundation of health IT standards that are agreed upon by all important stakeholders. Further, given the complexity of the activities required to implement health IT and the large number of stakeholders, completing and implementing comprehensive planning activities are also key to ensuring program success. Finally, an overall privacy approach that ensures public confidence and trust is essential to successfully promoting the use and acceptance of health IT. Without further action taken to address these areas of concern, opportunities to achieve greater efficiencies and improvements in the quality of the nation's health care may not be realized.

This concludes my statement. I would be pleased to answer any questions that you or other Members of the Committee may have.

Contacts and Acknowledgments

If you should have any questions about this statement, please contact me at (202) 512-6304 or by e-mail at melvinv@gao.gov. Other individuals who made key contributions to this statement are Barbara S. Collier, Heather A. Collins, Amanda C. Gill, Linda T. Kohn, Rebecca E. LaPaze, and Teresa F. Tucker.

160

Appendix E

GAO's Mission	The Government Accountability Office, the audit, evaluation, and investigative arm of Congress, exists to support Congress in meeting its constitutional responsibilities and to help improve the performance and accountability of the federal government for the American people. GAO examines the use of public funds; evaluates federal programs and policies; and provides analyses, recommendations, and other assistance to help Congress make informed oversight, policy, and funding decisions. GAO's commitment to good government is reflected in its core values of accountability, integrity, and reliability.
Obtaining Copies of GAO Reports and Testimony	The fastest and easiest way to obtain copies of GAO documents at no cost is through GAO's Web site (www.gao.gov). Each weekday afternoon, GAO posts on its Web site newly released reports, testimony, and correspondence. To have GAO e-mail you a list of newly posted products, go to www.gao.gov and select "E-mail Updates."
Order by Phone	The price of each GAO publication reflects GAO's actual cost of production and distribution and depends on the number of pages in the publication and whether the publication is printed in color or black and white. Pricing and ordering information is posted on GAO's Web site, http://www.gao.gov/ordering.htm. Place orders by calling (202) 512-6000, toll free (866) 801-7077, or TDD (202) 512-2537. Orders may be paid for using American Express, Discover Card, MasterCard, Visa, check, or money order. Call for additional information.
To Report Fraud, Waste, and Abuse in Federal Programs	Contact: Web site: www.gao.gov/fraudnet/fraudnet.htm E-mail: fraudnet@gao.gov Automated answering system: (800) 424-5454 or (202) 512-7470
Congressional Relations	Ralph Dawn, Managing Director, dawnr@gao.gov, (202) 512-4400 U.S. Government Accountability Office, 441 G Street NW, Room 7125 Washington, DC 20548
Public Affairs	Chuck Young, Managing Director, youngc1@gao.gov, (202) 512-4800 U.S. Government Accountability Office, 441 G Street NW, Room 7149 Washington, DC 20548

Index

Index

Index

Conflict avoidance behaviors, 18
Congruence with organizational
    models and strategic
    partners, 105
Contingency planning, importance
    of, 24
Contracts, vendor, 37
    performance expectations
    included in, 38
Critical thinking, perspectives in, 105
Cultures, merging healthcare system
    and university, 53–56

Data aggregation
    for quality assessment and
    improvement, 67
    for research, 73
Data capture, 124
Data centers
    protection from downtime in,
    21–26
    remote secondary, 24
    as single points of failure, 23
Data mining for quality assessment,
    66–67
Decision-making processes,
    outcomes driving duration
    and method of, 45
Decision support integrated
    documentation, 68
Delay in project implementation
    failure of project having timely
    start vs., 17
    frustration of end users caused
    by, 45
Design parameters, development by
    too few users of, 74
Device selection, mobile nursing, 43–46
Documentation devices
    PDA-based, 83–87
    point of care, 43–46

Downtime
    CPOE and medication error for,
    33–38
    as critical issue in healthcare, 36
    data center, 21–26
    drills recommended for HIT, 37
    of EHR system, 97
    of pharmacy, 34–35
Due diligence for vendor claims, 62–63

Electronic health record (EHR) system
    for ambulatory care, 59–63
    CCHIT standards for, 69
    clinical adoption of, 77–82
    community-based, 77–82
    community health center, 65–70
    costs of, planning for and
    understanding total, 79
    custom-developed, 65–75
    enterprise integrated, 95–99
    enterprise strategy needed in, 61
    financial components of, testing
    requirements for, 53–56
    goals for, 93
    integration of components in, 98
    labor-saving capabilities of, 67
    learning from past mistakes in
    implementing, 79–80
    maintenance plan for, 132
    meaningful use of, as incentive
    under ARRA, 92, 93
    organizational cultures affecting
    planning and implementation
    of, 53–56
    people skills essential to
    successful, 127–36
    phased implementation of, 81
    replacement of, 47–51
    in small practice, 89–93
    text files attached to, 97
    underuse of features of, 89–93

Index

Electronic medication administration record (eMAR)
medication dosage errors in, 27–29
objectives vs. project timelines in implementing, 9–14
postimplementation problems of, 11–13
rollout of, 11, 13
support necessary for, 11, 12
vendor planning with interdisciplinary team for, 10
training for, 11
ePharmacy, political support for, 30
Errors, resources studying, 120
Executive sponsor of project, 14
Experts, comparing advice of local and outside, 56

Failure mode analysis, 37, 38
Fire alarm system failure, 22, 24, 25
Fit of information and communication technologies with contextual issues, 105
Flexibility of leadership in response to project failure, 50

Gap analysis, 81
prior to product selection, 62
Go-live, definition of, 13
Goals
failure to list and track project, 84
reconciling and managing participants', 85

Health information exchange, linking clinical systems for, 49
Health information, inputs to capture, 124

Health information management (HIM) professionals, EHR implementation as priority of, 127
Health information technology (HIT)
adoption of, *xvi*
barriers to, research in, 106
challenges for successful projects in, *xv*
expectations imposed on, 30
Health information technology (HIT) failure
definition of, *xvi*
gradations in, 91
interviews to determine causes of, 96
planning for, 41
rates of, *xvi*
reasons for lack of acceptance in, 74
review of, 103–7
risk of, 73
value of sharing cases of, *xvi,* 106–7
Health information technology (HIT) implementation
adjusting plan for evolving user needs in, 86–87
broad effects of poor, 56
expanding scope as common in, 69
foundation of, staff and financial resources as, 78
for individual patient records versus population-based reporting, 70
phased, 81
success factors for, 61
workflow analysis for, 121–25
Health information technology (HIT) projects
defining strategic goals and objectives conducive to success of, 56
examined for risk factors, 107

incorporating lessons learned into strategies and plans for, 107
phases of, 13
transparent discussions about, 18
Health information technology (HIT) system downtime, 33–38
Hospital care case studies, 1–56
  for clinical decision support systems, 15–19
  for CPOE implementation, 3–7
  for data center protection, 21–26
  for eMAR, 9–14
  for health information system suite replacement, 47–51
  for IT decision making, 53–56
  for mobile nursing devices, 43–46
  for nursing electronic documentation, 39–42
  for pharmacy system, 27–31, 33–38
HL7 interface messages for medication orders, 27–31
Human resources, 123

Informaticians, analysis of HIT issues by, 103–4
Informatics specialist, failure to use EHR implementation expertise of, 53–56
Informatics to build evidence from clinical practice, 68
Information and communications technology (ICT) professionals, 104
Information and communications technology (ICT) projects, 104–5
  lack of infusion of, 106
Information management paradigm, 128

Information systems for clinical care, changes required in introducing, 17
Information technology (IT) help desk, response time and staffing of, 11, 12
Information technology (IT), usability of, 123
Infrastructure for sharing patient data and information using EHR system, 77
Institutional setting, history, and structure, 105
Integrated medication management system, 10
Interdisciplinary informatics governance, 18
Interface, system, relearning evolving, 85
Interrelationships among key organizational components and groups, 105–6
Interviews to ensure values and approaches match applicant's expertise, 55–56

Leadership
  to define HIT performance criteria, 37, 38
  effective, impact of organizational culture for, 53–56
  for EHR system implementation, 59–63, 127, 128–29
  talented and committed, as critical project success factor, 61
Logoff, user, 96

"Magic bullet" theory of IT, 106
Manual medical record keeping and procedures, reversion to, 24

Index

Repetition of past implementation errors, 79–80

Reports, custom software designed for quality, 65–70

"Required competencies," 39–42

Research case studies and analyses, resources giving examples of, 118–19

Resource allocations, ensuring adequate project, 85–86

Rogers' Diffusion of Innovation, 104

Root cause analysis of medication administration error, 34

Safety expectations for HIT and management, 36

Scaling narrow successful project to more courses, users, and needs, failure in, 85

Servers
automatic shutdown of data center, 21–26
dial-up modem access to data on, 66

Single-vendor strategy for software suites, 47–51

Small practice use of EHR system
customization not implemented in, 90
efficiency and effective charge capture as reasons for adoption in, 89
ePrescribing and CPOE in, 90, 91
failure to update software versions in, 90
rules reconfigurations ignored in, 90
security practices as lax in, 90

Social informatics (SI) principles, 104

Sociotechnical issues revealed by system implementation, 98, 99

Sociotechnical theory, 104

Software projects
abandoned, 61
custom EHR, 65–75
delayed delivery in, 95
research rules applied in, 68
specifications for, failure to meet, 95
testing platform for, early and aggressive, 86

Staff partnership, clinical, administrative, and IT, 61

Staffing, hospital, effects on training programs of, 40

Stakeholders
brainstorming with, 122
identifying and involving all, 62, 63, 74, 80–81, 82, 129
input from, as insufficient to ensure success of innovation, 87
underrepresented, 73, 97, 98

Standardized terminologies for EHR data, 65–70

Student patient record (SPR) programs, 83–87

Success factors, 105

Support for system use, ongoing, 78, 130

Surgeon resistance to EHR system data access features, 97

Sustainability of HIT projects, resource for, 120

System performance monitoring, 39

System updates not installed, 84

Technical features causing user resistance to EHR system, 96–97

Technology
fear of job loss due to, 130